CLARE OF ASSISI

A Mythological Study

Barbara Faris

Fisher King Publishing

Clare of Assisi
ISBN 978-1-910406-02-1
Copyright © Barbara Faris 2014

Published by
Fisher King Publishing
The Studio
Arthington Lane
Pool-in-Wharfedale
LS21 1JZ
England

Cover design by
Rick Armstrong

Contents

The Myth of Clare of Assisi:
A Medieval Woman for the Twenty-first Century

Part I

Part II

Sister Barbara Faris OSF

Barbara's greatest boast is that she is the daughter of a small-town, neighborhood barkeeper. She lived above the bar and helped in a tiny kitchen preparing fish fries, chicken dinners, hamburgers and steak-burgers. It is there that she learned about the care of community from parents who outwardly swam in the river of Dionysian Mysteries  and inwardly walked on the waters of deep faith.

The Sisters of St. Francis built upon their 'earthy' spirituality. Her Franciscan community developed the discipline needed for a life of contemplation in the midst of fifty years in active service. She taught in elementary and Junior High, educated the laity in the post Vatican II Church, worked among people in the inner city and the Native American communities, and was chaplain in hospital and hospice settings. All these eventually led her to study Clare, considered by some scholars to be co-foundress of the Franciscan way of life.

St. Clare, as she is named in Catholic circles, models Greek mythology wedded to the experience and leadership style of the 21st Century woman. She bespeaks the meaning of Catholic - 'from among the people'. She walks among us and needs only to be recognized. This study may help in the endeavor.

Foreword
'Transformed people transform'

These words of Richard Rohr resonate throughout the life of Clare of Assisi who, with her friend Francis, undermined the Feudal System of her times and modeled an attitude toward life which introduced women to their gifts. She founded communities, and advanced a Form of Life which focused on self-determination and communal decision making. Her 'Rule' was the first Form of Life written by a woman for women to be accepted by the Catholic Church.

This study is not theological, nor aimed solely at Catholic readers. Its purpose is twofold - to develop the story of mythology itself as a viable academic study, and to incarnate/enflesh the woman Clare. Hopefully those who are already introduced to Clare and those who have never heard of her will find food for thought and ongoing study from this perspective of her life. History lives in the mind but humanity lives in the imagination. Mythology, psychology, history and literature join forces in uncovering her character.

Part One offers an academic infrastructure for a more subjective presentation of Clare found in the second section. Part Two employs the senses metaphorically to support predominant themes in the spirituality of Clare.

Welcome to the Odyssey.

Dedication

For all who seek the simple way of life no
matter their religious tradition, spirituality,
culture or economic status.

In gratitude to the staff of Fisher King
Publishing, particularly Samantha Richardson,
Carol Butler and Rick Armstrong.

Part I

Introduction and Background

I am a Roman Catholic Franciscan sister. For forty-five years I have endeavored to understand the way of Francis of Assisi, and only within the last five years have I discovered Clare of Assisi, the feminine soul mate of Francis. At this juncture in life, the desire to 'know' her has replaced 'knowing about' her. The tale of my first meeting outside of the box of Catholic legends encircling this thirteenth-century mystic demands telling, for without it there would be no dissertation and this book would not exist. It is the center through which this odyssey progresses and gains the momentum to move from the past and into the present in a continuous motion of exchange.

She Came Unannounced

The challenge of choosing such a topic was forefront in my conscious life after completing an MA in Mythological Studies, and being accepted for on-going PhD work. I was intrigued by Stephen Aizenstat, president of Pacifica Graduate Institute, who comments on the Institute's "imaginal perspective" in his introductory essay to the collection entitled *Depth Psychology: Meditations in the Field*. Describing the history of the institute from its inception in 1974 through to the present, Aizenstadt expresses its challenging opportunity to connect art with science, poetry with information, and imagination with cognition. Writing a dissertation in the atmosphere of this open minded intellectual pursuit presents the student with a variety of possibilities for topics. However, Aizenstadt limits the field in stating what he believes concerning this endeavor. He reflects:

"Pacifica is most interested in the imaginal perspective-seeing through visible content to the invisibles of imagination; how does one write a dissertation from that perspective? Not only does the topic call the person, but the person goes into her own experience and wonders how she is affected by the topic. When the person and the topic come into relation, the other possibilities emerge. Dreams also contribute, offering that subtle body experience which lies beyond the personal and beyond the story line."

It is out of the imaginal perspective that the topic of this dissertation emerged. Therefore, it contains narrations of the imaginal experiences which birthed its writing. However, unlike the suggestion by Aizenstadt, the movement will not be "… seeing through the visible to the invisibles of the imagination." It will move from seeing through the invisibles of the imagination into the visible of the physical world, in that the topic discussed is a woman who made herself known to me, uninvited and unexpected, in an imaginal vision. Following is the setting and background of this experience.

Soon to begin PhD classes, I needed to move to another city. In the process of the move and in the midst of choosing a dissertation topic, a character dramatically emerged from out of my unconscious. She was swift in coming and abrupt in exiting. She remained stamped in my consciousness with indelible ink. Skeptical of such ethereal experiences, I wondered at how real she appeared and how struck I was by her unexpected emergence. "Forget it. You're just tired and dreamy," said I to myself. However, the woman would not be forgotten. She glued herself to my mind like a barnacle on the underside of a boat. I could not avoid her.

The image of the woman in blue jeans, as I call her, invaded my psyche. She companioned my waking state with a plaintive, knowing smile. Gaston Bachelard emphasizes the powerful energy embedded in waking imagining in an essay entitled, 'Reading as a Dimension of Consciousness,' included in the book *On Poetic Imagination and Reverie*. He reflects that, "Reverie gathers being around its dreamer … Reverie lives on in its initial interest. The subject is astonished to encounter the image in his reverie: indeed, he is amazed, charmed, awakened."

An image contains a unique inner power. Bachelard remarks, "Suddenly an image occupies the heart of our imagining being. It seizes us, holds us. It infuses us with being." Like a past popular tune, the image of the woman in blue jeans returned to my mind, "You keep coming back like a song, a song that keeps saying remember."

"Remember what?" my beleaguered brain wondered. Finally, giving full attention of my consciousness to the phenomenon, I stopped and asked, "Who is this woman? What does she want of me?" I decided to find out. Thus began this journey.

Who is this Woman?

Clare of Assisi, foundress of the Poor Ladies of San Damiano, died in 1253, leaving as a parting message to the women who followed her: "Tend your soul and the souls of your sisters." What might this mean in the twenty-first century, when the emphasis of human striving shifts toward tending the earth? Ecologists, social justice advocates, and concerned scientists question the use and abuse of earth's resources and seek solutions to sustaining the natural environment of this world. When is enough, enough? To whom does the earth belong? Does earth *belong* to anyone?

Does earth, like Clare's sister, have a soul to be tended and cherished?

Pacifica Graduate Institute seeks to attend to the world as a living organism which sustains all life. The Institute incorporates this principle into its motto *anima mundi colendai gratia* - for the sake of tending the soul of the world. Clare of Assisi offers a microcosmic model of this same macrocosmic ideal to care for the universe as it is present in the twenty-first century.

Clare of Assisi (1193-1253) saw the need of tending soul eight hundred years ago. Focusing on the human soul, she refused to call anything her own. Her attitude of seeing through into the abundance of creation overrides that of looking at the scarcity of resources, as she stoutly refused to accept the possessive posturing of the culture and church of her time. Clare saw poverty to be a privilege, becoming the standard around which her style of communal life rallied. Clare concentrated her laser sights on the vision that *all* is gift - gift from the giver of all, the source of all creation, whom she envisioned as *the gift*. God as gift undergirded her ideal of poverty. Clare's unique understanding of poverty as gift will be discussed further in this study. Its import in the present context lies in Clare's encircling of all creation in a compassionate embrace. Her compassion encompasses all creation, beginning with the community closest to her, her sisters at the enclosure known as San Damiano. It is this seeing-through, inclusive vision of creation and its ramifications on her society which constitute part of her genius. The challenge of uncovering this genius eight hundred years after her death presents its own problems of academic approach, demanding a fresh look at Clare and her history. The mode of entrance is a matter of the spirit and the spirit of the matter. Both need a say. One means is through prayer.

The manner of entering the realm of the spirit which I know and practice is the art of prayer. Within the context of connecting with the spiritual, I chat with angels and saints. This is no ecstatic and visionary experience. It is more akin to C. G. Jung's active imagining as described by J. Marvin Spiegelman in a lecture included in the text, *Jungian Psychology and the Passions of the Soul.* Spiegelman comments:

"Jung, you will recall, made a strict distinction between active imagination and art. The former was aimed at the reaction of the personality rather than towards works of art. One must clearly find a balance between the need for understanding and the aesthetic need in such an endeavor. In his *Memoirs,* Jung tells us how he was tempted by a siren feminine voice, both inner and outer, who told him that his work was "art." He manfully resisted that insinuation and persuaded himself - and us - that his work was in the interest of science. What was needed was for the person to understand and transform himself ..."

It is on the stage of active imagination at the service of personal transformation that this dissertation plays out its saga. Not conceived in a daydream of my invention, but more as an experience of being pushed beyond the limits of my own dreams, I hope to understand and be transformed by seeking to know this woman. The following story, unlike a conscious choice of prayer, constitutes a description of the inception of this dissertation.

She Appears: The Story

I slump into an antiquated, overstuffed chair. The scent of coffee fills the air. Young furrow-browed students crouch over books strewn atop beat-up tables, concentrating in spite of the loud music and musty surroundings. Paintings of questionable quality thrust themselves on my tired eyes. The wavy lines of a woman's torso adorned solely with fuzzy pubic hair silences the imagination in its graphic portrayal. Little was left to the imagination. I was much too tired for that to bother me. Another portrait of faces scowling from a black background, mouths drawn downward and eye-orbs staring rigidly open into whatever space remains in the cluttered environment. Bone weary from the latest of my geographical moves, the late afternoon caffeine rush would see me through a night of unpacking boxes. In that place and at that time, she appears.

A thin woman of middle years, dressed in blue jeans, a tee shirt, and tennis shoes, medium length, grey-brown hair drawn back from her face, sits with one leg slung over the arm rest of an overstuffed chair opposite me. She gazes straight into my eyes. I smile back. Then she is gone from the place... but not from my psyche.

The Way In

After her first appearance, the reverie remained with me as I unpacked my boxes. I needed to find out more about this visitor, but how to access her? As previously described, I employed some of what C. G. Jung named "active imagination" in the context of prayer as I connected with the invisible spiritual powers which are in the Catholic tradition known as angels and saints. However, such communication was guided and circumscribed by two centuries of well-defined boundaries of spiritual interpretation and a process known as the "discernment of spirits," a sometimes lengthy process employed when life changing decisions are to be reached in a person's life. This process serves to distinguish 'good/holy spirits' from 'bad /evil spirits,' and even from 'misguiding spirits.' This visit did not fit the criterion for such a process. It interrupted my life only insofar as causing me to wonder. Mystery, not duality and confusion, hovered around this image. I turned to depth psychology for further guidance in order to find a way to communicate with this bared part of the unconscious; a way to make it discernible to consciousness. Spirit longed for materialization, but how?

Approaches: Awakening Consciousness

A method of connection manifested itself in the writings on psycho-mythology. This process of interaction is explained and employed by J. Marvin Spiegelman who describes it as a new literary genre, "...in which an individual's fantasy transcends the personal level, reaching the collective unconscious," and "...is connected with either available religious or mythical material and is clearly intended as a work of art" (ii).

In his book *The Tree* (1974), Spiegelman navigates the perilous waters of exemplifying his own method by sharing the stories from his life's journey. Spiegelman dialogues with the images appearing from his unconscious. In the later book, *Jungian Psychology and the Passions of the Soul* (1989), Spiegelman expands on the personal aspects of transformation, contending that the individuation process is a gift to the collective. He holds up the individual's process of transformation to the gaze of the collective other, through the eyes of the arts. Spiegelman allows the images of the psyche a life of their own. Like Jung, he uses the "temptation by the feminine siren, art," as an invitation to transcend the boundaries of art and science. Jung later refers to this action as the Transcendent Function. This function creates a new inclusive symbol which embodies a means of bridging matter and spirit, using the mind as the interpreter: a bridge strong enough to support the physical and psychology, the passions and the intellect. This newly created symbol is to be taken seriously enough to allow it to help us discover a way to materialize its life into a subjective reality with which to relate and communicate. It is this objective of psycho-mythology which lends itself to connecting with the image of the woman in blue jeans.

Spiegelman builds upon Jung's ideas, noting that after sixteen years of working with active imagination as modelled by Jung, he discovered "that the figures of my own active imagination now wanted to tell stories about their own quests and experiences, desiring my cooperation in this venture" (Spiegelman vi). As Jung discovered a way to deal with the passions, which he called Active Imagination, Spiegelman enters the territory of the unconscious, and dialogues with its inhabitants within the dimension of giving the images lives of their own. The "imaginer" is beckoned beyond his/her own psyche into the collective psyche. The personal psyche is invited to investigate the image in a context greater than its Self. Strong passions in partnership with the Self lead to where one "allows the emotion to fill my being," and proceed to inquire into "how it looks, what it intends" (Spiegelman). Life finds a home in the image, and the image a home in matter. However, Jung and Spiegelman are not the only scholars interested in the concept of the living image as possessing a life of its own. There is more to be said about the symbol of the woman in blue jeans and her claim on the territory called, "a life of my own".

Images that Live

Gaston Bachelard, beguiled by the concept of a living image, insists on its propensity to materialize. He suggests in the essay, "Matter is Dreamed and Not Perceived":

"Since reverie is always considered in terms of a relaxed consciousness, one usually ignores dreams of definite action, which I will designate as reveries of will... We will therefore have to pay strict attention if we wish to understand the prospective activity of images, if we want to give the image its place even before perception, as a forerunner of perception."*(On Poetic Imagination*, 12-14)

The woman appeared while I was in a state of relaxation. I was resting and awake, thus according to Bachelard's reckoning, this was not a "reverie of will." Listening was paramount, since the image clung to my mind. It was not a question of my choosing to place the image before the perception. Not percepted, it appeared of its own volition like a stranger in the night. She was new to me. My dreams I could interpret. She was a different phenomenon. Shored up by the findings of Spiegelman and Bachelard, I decided to go the way of active imagination following the approach suggested by Spiegelman's psycho-mythology and Bachelard's "prepercepted" image. I would choose to go inside myself, call back our first meeting, and have a chat with this blue-jeaned woman.

Close Encounters of the Psycho-mythological Kind

The first encounter and chat developed as follows: I go inside and down. Seated on the sand by the sea, it's sunny and warm. A large serpent comes out of the water, sniffs my face like a cat and goes on its way. I look to my right. The woman is seated on a log. She calls me to sit by her. I go. We are seated on the log with me, and as I gaze in wonder at her, she smiles. I notice that her eyes are blue and more brightly crystaline and bluer as I look into them. She becomes solemn as she gazes into my eyes. I ask her what the look means. She says that I already know. Then she says that I treat her as if she does not exist - like the *Let's Pretend* stories on the radio when I was a child.

I recall my favorite story from the radio broadcast. The story was called "The Selfish Giant." In the story, the giant is tamed by a lonely child who wanders into the giant's garden. The giant lifts the child up in his huge hands. I can hear the child suck in air as the giant lifts him up for a closer look. The giant befriends the lonely child. One day the child shows up hurt and bleeding and the giant roars, "Who has dared to wound thee?"

This all passes through my mind in an instant. I want to say something but find nothing to say. Confused, I ask why the woman comes to me dressed as she is. She says she is in comfortable clothes for work and play. I then ask her name. She responds that I already know her name and reminds me of the time when, driving from Ventura to Santa Barbara, I identified the feminine spirits most present to me by naming them: Mary Mary, Mary Aphrodite, Mary Hestia, Mary Artemis, Mary Barbara, Mary Agnes, Mary Theresa. I laugh and ask which Mary she is. She responds, "Mary Barbara." I then fall into a deep sleep.

My second encounter takes place a day later. I am conscious and aware of what I am about to do. There is no sense of the ephemeral or other worldly.

I go inside and down. I am back in the coffee shop. The woman is seated across from me as when I first saw her. She remains friendly. I ask who she is. She responds that I already know. I become angry, expressing my frustration at her response. I tell her that I am flesh and blood. She is vague and appears at unexpected times and places. How can she expect that I "already know her?" I feel my stomach cramp up. The woman says that it is best if I calm down for the moment. The kindness in her face and voice calm me. I listen. She explains that she IS woman, my feminine, and holds all that is woman within me. She explains that I can name which woman-ness she is for me at any given time. From outside, I hear my neighbor, Dee, calling to another neighbor. "I'm lonely," she declares. I laughingly comment that I prefer not to identify my inner woman as Dee. I wait and listen as I look at the woman and she looks at me. Then I utter, "You are Clare." She smiles. I notice that her pulled-back hair gives her an appearance of commonness. I feel that I can trust her. I tell her that I am uncertain about my dissertation topic and scared that I will not be able to finish it. I feel alone in the venture. I begin to sob, tears suddenly welling up. Clare says how well she knows the fear of being a lone outsider. How fully she experienced it by moving beyond the protection of the city walls, completely vulnerable to wild men and wild nature. As for uncertainty - there were nights she spent begging God just to know what she was to do the next moment. She said that in spite of having companions, desire filled her with loneliness. Through my tears I respond that I have no companions. Clare reminds me of my many companions and names them. I am not alone and never will be alone.

We are suddenly at the ocean shore. We are sitting on logs facing one another, her blue eyes so full of love that I begin to weep again. Clare takes me in her arms and I sob on her shoulder. I then become aware that I am sitting by myself expelling a deep sigh. All is calm with a sense of peace. I feel relieved.

On the conscious level: since this visitation, knowing Clare of Assisi has become my passion. Forty-five years as a professed Franciscan sister had not brought me close to this woman who in the twelfth century introduced a style of communal living based on total dependence upon God as she understood God. The Biblical Gospels centering on an experience of God in the person of the historical Jesus Christ formed and permeated her understanding of God. It is not the intent of this study to question or argue about Clare's philosophy and theology. My questions are: Can her myth be revisioned so as to speak to the people of the twenty-first century? Does her life contribute to the on-going movement of women toward claiming their own place and dignity in the story of humankind? Is her way too radical to be practical in modern society? Is her belief that all human beings are mystics a practical idea for a.time in history when technology predominates?

I discovered for certain that Clare of Assisi would be the topic of my dissertation. Beyond that inner assurance, little else formed by way of articulating objectively what the meaning and purpose of such a pursuit would entail. It lay before me to move through the beginnings of this odyssey into personal transformation studied through the lens of the collective unconscious, and portrayed in the life of Clare of Assisi.

Chapter One
Entrances into the Study

The Door of Hagiography

The intent of this dissertation is to approach the study of Clare of Assisi from a mythological point of view, grounded in depth psychology. However, in order to proceed, it is necessary to draw a distinction between myth and the Catholic tradition of storytelling known as hagiography. The life of Clare of Assisi, a Roman Catholic Nun whose life spanned the years 1193 through 1256, has found written expression in the inspirational stories contained in the tales formed to introduce the members of her order to the exemplary lives of persons considered to be models of virtue, as viewed by the Roman Catholic Church.

Hagiography, a word derived from the Greek *hagios,* meaning holy, aims at expressing the Catholic Church's understandings of what living a holy life entails. Hagiographical stories elaborate on the events in a person's life in a way designed to inspire the faithful of its tradition to emulate the virtues manifested in the lives of the saints. Vices, mistakes, and imperfections are alluded to in order to reinforce the image of perfection to which the saints aspired, especially women saints. These stories are written to encourage believers to find strength to live a good and holy life as envisioned by the Catholic tradition of understanding such a life. The written word, as demonstrated by the suffix *graphy,* transmits the stories through written expression, although the stories were originally shared among the believers through dialogue and oral tradition. Furthermore, hagiography tells the story of a given person, in most cases a canonized or ritually proclaimed saint, in order to lead the reader to a given conclusion that such a life patterns a style of a good life which leads to God, aiming at a moral to be taught and virtue to be emulated.

Is the hagiographical story of Clare a myth? Before venturing into the mythological study proposed for this dissertation, it is necessary to draw some distinctions between hagiography and myth in order to clarify the mythological approaches that will be employed in its writing.

Butler's *Lives of the Saints,* a hagiographical compilation of better-known saints in the Roman Catholic Tradition, represents Clare of Assisi as a full-fledged saint of extraordinary virtue. In it, Clare is described as follows:

The Lady Clare, shining in name, more shining in life, most shining in conversation, was a native of Assisi, of noble birth and by grace nobler, a maiden most pure in heart, young in years but hoary in determination, most steadfast in purpose, but withal wise and meek and a marvellous lover of Christ. She was born about the year 1193. Her mother was Ortolana di Fiumi and her father Faverone Offreduccio, and she had a younger sister, Agnes, and another, Beatrice, but of her childhood, adolescence and home life there are no certain facts. When she was eighteen St. Francis came to preach the Lenten sermons at the church of San Giorgio in Assisi: his words fired her, she sought him out secretly, and asked him to help her that she too might live "after the manner of the holy gospel."

Francis spoke to her of contempt for the world, the joys and graces of service to others emphasizing the love of God. He further strengthened her nascent desire to leave all things for Christ. Therefore, on Palm Sunday in the year 1212 Clare attended at the cathedral of Assisi for the blessing of palms; when all the rest went up to the altar rails to receive their olive branch Clare remained in her place. The bishop noticed, so he went from the altar down to her and gave her the branch. In the evening she ran away from home and went a mile out of the town to the Portiuncula, where St. Francis lived with his little community. He and his brethren met her at the door of the chapel of our Lady of the Angels with lighted tapers in their hands. It is there where she exchanged her rich clothing for the penitential habit of sackcloth tied round the waist with a cord, after which St. Francis cut off her hair, and Francis, not having as yet any nunnery prepared for her, placed her in the Benedictine convent of St. Paul near Bastia, where she was affectionately received. It would seem that the relatives of St. Clare (her father was probably dead) had proposed a particular marriage that did not recommend itself to her, but that she did not entirely renounce the idea of matrimony in general until the burning words of Francis persuaded her to commit her maidenhood finally to God. Then followed what G. K. Chesterton called this "regular romantic elopement, in which the bridegroom was Christ and St. Francis the 'knight errant' who gave it a happy ending."

In this study, hagiography will be made use of only to show how the historical story was passed on through the last eight hundred years of Catholic tradition. Philosophical and theological considerations are outside the parameters of this study. Depth psychology, through its integration of myths, archetypes, and shadow, undergirds the mythological approaches which will be employed in this study. The dark realms in the struggle to be human find a home in depth psychology. This fact will be of prime importance when uniting the spirit/matter and saint/human who lives in the person of Clare of Assisi. I will return to this story in a later chapter. Within the present context, it suffices to exemplify a style of storytelling which will not be employed in this study, but which offers a first glimpse of Clare of Assisi.

The Door of Mythological Scholarship

Mythology takes a variety of forms, from legends to fairy tales, from folk tales to stories which focus on god and goddess. Thomas J. Sienkewicz, editor of a two volume annotated bibliography entitled *Theories of Myth and World Mythologies* respectively, alerts the reader early in the introduction, warning that:

"The study of myth presents special problems of definition, because the semantic range of the English word "myth" tends to be inclusive rather than exclusive. The ambiguity of the word began in ancient Greek where the word *mythos* could mean any "utterance, "speech", or "story."

William Doty, in his text *Mythography-the Study of Myths and Rituals*, quotes Albert Cook as saying, "Language is haunted, and the act of defining myth is an act of something like exorcism." Doty goes on to give his own seventeen-point definition of the word, adding more demons to be explored and expelled in order to uncover the elusive quality in the word, *myth*.

Mythologists wrestle with pinning down a meaning only to find that myth slips out of every hold and each pinning. Carl Kerenyi offers a simpler description concerning the delusive propensity of myth. He states: "The word 'myth' is altogether too equivocal, blunted, and hazy for our purposes; it does not give us as much of a start as the expressions (in Greek) meaning 'to put together,' 'to say.'" (Kerenyi, C. and Jung, C. G., *Essays on a Science of*

Mythology, 2-3).

The purposes to which Kerenyi refers in this quote dwell in myth's and mythology's contributions to the study of origins, and how this study illuminates a pathway for one's own investigations in the field of mythology. Kerenyi poses that "to put together" and "to say" are only starting points.

Other scholars have had a say as to what myth and mythology might be. Most do not hazard definitions but settle upon descriptions. Linda Sexton, after an experience of creating an "un-Christmas" play for a group of "secularized, rational-humanist Unitarians," reports in her book, *Ordinarily Sacred,* that "myth is a symbolic narrative that gives order to chaos, truth to tales...". Sexton encouraged the children to create an original Christmas story not harkening to the Bethlehem version. In the process she discovered that according to her understanding, the myth written by the youths did what myths have always done, "...it merged depth and daylight and bestowed a new order on the chaos of both."

Christine Downing chooses a more personal approach to picturing myth. She views myth as the teacher itself. In the book, *The Goddess: Mythological Images of the Feminine* she comments, "Truly to know these myths means recognizing ourselves in them. One learns about myth from myth - from the discovery of what it means to live a myth." On the other hand, Michael Grosso, author of an extensive study of the twenty-first century millennium phenomenon in his book *The Millennium Myth: Love and Death at the End of Time,* writes a new myth. Gross suggests that technology and virtual reality are the builders of the myth of modern humans. As an exercise in the use of a limited description of myth in today's world, Gross envisions myth as, "...both a source of guiding light and a caster of sinister shadows... I focus on the visionary power of the Myth - one man's reconnaissance report."

Descriptions which offer a more scientific, empirical evaluation of myth include those put forward by Samuels, Shorter, and Plaut in their resource for psychoanalysis, *A Critical Dictionary of Jungian Analysis*. They offer background for the meaning which Jung gives to myth, and then warn:

"There is also a danger in taking myth literally. Myth is analogous to certain aspects of personal experience but it cannot be seen as a substitute without consequent INFLATION. It provides a metaphorical perspective, but isn't an explication or a portent to be fulfilled. It is a non-personal image which provides psychic space for individual expression."

Jung takes myth into the divine/spiritual realm. Myth, seen in the context of the human experience of the cosmos at a given time in history, has the capability of helping humankind to find meaning. Jung equates meaninglessness with illness. Jung concludes that biological science reinforces the idea that homo sapiens could become extinct as evidenced by the demise of other species (340). Unless meaning is found by a cooperating effort of the conscious and the unconscious, a like fate may await humankind. Jung gives myth the distinguished place of helpmate in finding meaning and concludes in the chapter entitled "Late Thoughts" at the end of *Memories, Dreams, Reflections,* that:

"No science will ever replace myth, and a myth cannot be made out of any science. For it is not that "God" is a myth, but that myth is the revelation of a divine life in man.

It is not we who invent myth, rather it speaks to us as a Word of God... It is not affected by the arbitrary operation of our will. We cannot explain an inspiration."

David Miller re-echoes Jung's belief that myth bestows upon humankind that which science and technology cannot: that is, meaning which may grace modern humankind with the understanding needed for moving into the future. Miller, in a short article included in the November/ December 1999 issue of *The Salt Journal,* grapples with the underside of the modern world society. The potential destructive force of technology unattended by wisdom is clearly evidenced as Miller lists the catastrophic events that have occurred worldwide in recent generations. He wonders what will offer insight on the significance of these dark and threatening events. Miller insists:

"Now what is crucial, crucial for the survival of our race and planet, has little to do with information and data, with sound bites or megabytes [...] Myths are not sound bites, not even megabytes of meaning, they are plots emplotting connections. [...] Mythology gives the understanding we now so desperately need if we are to survive at the end to the millennium in order to experience richly the next."

The Door of This Writer
What twist in the snaking road of myth's slithering elusiveness beckons this writer? After four and one half years of following the academic river of Mythological Studies with Emphasis on Depth Psychology at Pacifica Graduate Institute, I come to where it empties into a sea which I am to traverse alone, using all the remembrance of life's experiences and learning to shore up the courage to sail wherever this dissertation leads. Progressing further

demands its own understanding of myth; 'a myth of myth' as woven throughout this writing, didactic in character, yet nonetheless an image, for written word is also an image.

Mythology is a study of humankind in story form. Wrapped in the trappings of space, time, and traditions, it embodies the thoughts and desires of the world of human endeavor. It is a universal language repeating enduring questions, acting as a vessel for transporting the mind over the seas of history and into the ports of diverse cultures. It draws the reader to reflect upon humankind's deepest questions: Where do we come from? Where are we going? Why is there pain in the process of living? What is good? What is evil? Why do good people suffer? What is the meaning in life? Does life have a purpose?

Mythology does not answer questions. It does not pose them in objective articulation, because it is the science of the art of story weaving. Stories do not answer questions. Stories describe human experiences which are as diverse as the humans who create them. Within the tapestry of each myth or story are woven deeper images as true as the first apparent picture, which invites the seeker into the hidden images which thread into underlying images which undermine habitual thought and rigid expectations of daily living. Like the image within the image within the image in a room of mirrors, myths reflect back snapshots that are endemic to but separate from the imaginer. The myth coaxes new questions; queries based upon fresh insights developed through narrating a story which contains layers of meaning and interpretational possibilities.

Stories capture the human imagination. It is mythology which holds the vast collection of the human stories, making them accessible to the person as a unique individual and to the community as a secure society.

Mythology insists that the human species not take itself too seriously, allowing the human being to be a vessel of ongoing creativity. Although not conscious of it, children through the ages recognize the fun in myth. In the middle years of the twentieth century, a popular song echoed through the homes of America. In it, a child prods her elder to carry through on a societal event practiced through the ages, insisting that her elder, "Tell me a story, tell me a story, tell me a story, remember what you said. Tell me a story, tell me a story, tell me a story, before I go to bed."

Offering answers to enduring questions is not in the realm of mythology; however, facing those questions head-on is in its domain. It leads to a questioning gaze and reflective wonder. The tenor of mythology's questioning reverberates with open-minded melody. Not moralizing and defining, mythology tells a story which whets the imagination and leads the listener and reader to a reflective investigation of images. Bypassing mental gymnastics and fabricated thought systems it dares to enter into the world of the unanswerable, the tenuous, and the ambiguous; that is, the worlds of imagination, intuition, instinct, and play. This dissertation uses the lens of mythology to tell the story of a woman from medieval times whose myth appears in the hagiography of the Roman Catholic Church and whose influence changed the future of women religious in the Roman Catholic Church and in the economic and political world of her own time. Are her contributions significant in the world of the twenty-first century?

Mythology reaches into the earthy, instinctual and erratic behaviors of human beings in relation to "the gods" or spirits which are both human and beyond the human. Its stories call forth thought, wonder, and inquiry, challenging the reader to progress into the tales' multi-layered depths.

There is no effort to valorize good and holy behaviors. Its method is telling a story, manifesting every day, down to earth behaviors associated with the struggle to live in time and on this earth. Mythology tells about what is happening. It gives simple story to the 'is's' of life and uses the mode of telling a story to do just that - tell a story.   Anything beyond this is up to the reader/s.

The distinctions between myth and hagiography are apparent in their intent. In short, those intents can be listed as follows.

Hagiography	*Mythology*
Motivates to virtuous action	Narrates actions
Inspires to heroic deeds	Leads to reflection upon life
Implies/encourages moral judgement	Moral judgment not implicit to story
Focuses on human subjection to the divine	Focuses on interaction between human and divine
Is biographical	Can function as a psychology of the human mind
Judges the human condition	Descriptive of the human

Culturally, religiously particularized narratives	Culturally and religiously diverse narratives
Personal in scope/content	Personal in content and universal in application
Aims to inspire	Aims toward reflection and meaning

Hagiography, as a style of storytelling, mixes fact and fiction, which offers the reader a combination of the figurative and literal, and employs both to its own ends of inspiration and moralization according to a specific set of beliefs. On the other hand, mythology appears in a variety of forms. Some scholars make distinctions among myth, legends, fairy tales, and folk tales. Although there may sometimes be more practical lessons to be learned from the stories, the deepest quest is to broaden the spectrum of light around what it means to be human and what being human looks like in activities couched within stories. An open-minded stance characterizes the style of its search. Mythology is the chosen style of storytelling used in this dissertation.

Chapter Two
Myth Meets Mind

Mixed Messages

Clare and her friend Francis Bernadone together shook the feudal world of their times. They introduced an interpretation of the Christian Gospel which incorporated the value of total dispossession of all material security, both personal and communal. Their vision lived for eight hundred years in legends and inspirational writings. However, due to recent discoveries of authentic documents buried for centuries in the archives and libraries of European convents and monasteries, scholars within the Franciscan tradition are producing an avalanche of studies based upon these new findings. I will build upon the research of these women and men.

Clare Offreduccio is an historical person. The intent of this work is to exhume and re-envision the Clare of Assisi buried within eight hundred years of hagiography and history, this from a mythological point of view. Articulating a historical mythology or mythological history of Clare risks the violation of both history and mythology. The questions arise: "What is fact? and "What is fictive?"

The Fact of the Matter

Sources governing the historical facts specifically regarding Clare are scanty. Few of Clare's own writings are extant. Original writings referenced for this paper are based upon the research of Regis J. Armstrong, O.F.M. Cap., a present- day scholar in Franciscan Studies. As the editor and translator of the text *Clare of Assisi-Early Documents,* Armstrong synthesizes the discoveries of past scholars in introductions to each of the documents, thus placing them in the context of past and ongoing academic research. I expect to glean a knowledge of Clare based upon her own words. Eight documents constitute the totality of known writings by Clare. They include: the four letters addressed to Agnes of Prague between the years 1234 and 1253, Clare's Testament written between 1247 and 1253, the Rule of 1253, and the Blessing of 1253. Also included is *The Acts of the Process of Canonization*. The Process is a compilation of the testimony given to the clerical investigators gathered from persons who had direct contact with Clare and were willing to witness to her character. They are invaluable written documentation of information collected in the year 1253, just after her the death, and offer a picture of Clare as painted by those who daily encountered her.

The early biographers of Clare had fewer resources available to them than writers of today. Nesta de Robeck's biographical study of Clare predates many of today's endeavors to give credence to Franciscanism's contribution to the rational world of present- day academic scholarship. De Robeck's is clearly an act of love supported by scholarly resources available to her. She employs three of the authentic works of Clare to draw a well-rounded picture of the woman Clare. In her insightful study, *St. Clare of Assisi,* written in 1951, the bibliography of works cited includes selections in German, Italian, English, and Latin sources, indicating a breadth of knowledge not evident in other biographies, and a working knowledge of the four languages. It is also a good read. A 1995 biography by Sister Frances Teresa OSC (Order of St. Clare), *The Living Mirror,* looks at the Saint in relation to three themes: Conversion, Contrition, and Communion. The author's quoted excerpts of Clare's writings are her own translation from the Italian. It is a fine comparative study of the diversity of nuance present in translations. Some of her translations rather than Armstrong's will be employed in this paper.

Doing What Is Ours To Do: A Clarian Theology of Life is a compendium of theological reflections written by the present-day Poor Clares. In this collection edited by Margaret Eletta Guider OSF, women who live the enclosed life offer insights into the lived reality of Clare's message as experienced by them. These five essays are a first-time effort to pull together the diverse communal understandings of what Clare's vision looks like as lived by modern-day nuns. It marks a significant step forward in bringing Clare into the twenty-first century.

The Celebration of Clare's 800th Birthday, Clarefest, '93, brought an unexpected two thousand participants to the little campus of St. Rose of Viterbo College in La Crosse, Wisconsin. An eight-volume series, published to celebrate the birth of Clare of Assisi, entitled *Clare Centenary Series*, contains selected essays from presentations given at the Clarefest. Volume 8, published in 1996, addresses topics specific to Clare of Assisi in the medieval world. Their breadth of matter covered areas which I will be investigating in this dissertation: images of Clare, poverty, enclosure, fasting, and reformation movements, to name a few. This invaluable resource paints vignettes of thirteenth century culture, employing modern-day academic discoveries.

Margaret Carney is a Franciscan sister who specializes in Franciscan spiritual theology. While researching material on medieval women mystics, she was mystified at why Clare of Assisi went unmentioned for the most part. This led Carney on a quest which resulted in her dissertation, now in book form under the title *The First Franciscan Woman - Clare of Assisi and Her Form of Life.* Carney places Clare within the historical framework of the Friars Minor of Francis, and the medieval woman of central Italy in the twelfth and thirteenth centuries. Her research offers a style of intellectual investigation which takes into account Clare's feminine approach to one interpretation of the Franciscan charism. Carney investigates Clare's style of governance, understanding of poverty, insistence on mutual charity, and contribution to the Franciscan women of today. This book exemplifies a modern-day study which guides me on my own way toward seeking a Clare who speaks to modern women.

Clare of Assisi, A Biographical Study by Ingrid Peterson OSF, published in 1993, develops the life of Clare through a methodical and exhaustive examination of her personal friendships, surrounding culture, social contributions, and political environment. A diversity of modern research scholarship weaves its way through this extensive portrayal of the historical Clare. To date, it is the most broad and scholarly biographical study of Clare.

The matter of fact is not the only fact of the matter of this study. The fictive will have its say as well.

The "Fict" of the Matter

What of the fictive elements of this investigation? Can myth and history merge? It is evident that literature mixes the two in a creative dance step, "tripping the light fantastic" in a medley of poetic waltzes and prose fox trots. These are literary genres where poetic license gives reign to imagination. On the other hand, history, as understood by Western civilization, resembles the game of tinker toys. The bits and pieces are given, and the player builds a framework around which to mold a specific structure, filling in the spaces with factual information. In the sense of history, the builder creates the structure around a given framework.

On the other hand, mythology creates and recreates stories around the experience of being human. The story IS the structure. Anyone who has heard the same story twice or more knows that the teller freely adjusts events to fit the ears of the audience in order to tweak the attention and imagination of the listeners. Myth plays with facts, adding and subtracting for the sake of the story.

Historical, psychological, theological, and mythological are different ways of seeing. Can they be employed together without dishonoring the unique quality of each discipline? Can myth and other disciplines understand one another from a "seeing through" vantage point of a James Hillman? In what way might they share the same stage with a mythic Clare? Can mythology serve as the principal academic disciplinary lens which photographs Clare of Assisi?

Seeing Through the Mix

David Miller, in his book entitled *Hells and Holy Ghosts*, emphasizes the need to see through and beyond that which is already known. The book is Miller's own interpretation of that part of the Christian credo which claims belief in the death of Christ and his descent into hell. The book's introduction includes a quote from the diary of Mircea Eliade, chosen to re-enforce the notion that there is a way of penetrating truth which leads to personal transformation. In the introduction, Miller quotes Eliade as saying:

"The meaning of my "learning": I grasp the true

meaning only after having gone through all the material (enormous, inert, sombre documentation). [...] Drowned in the documents, what is personal, original, living in me disappears, dies. When I find myself again, when I return to life - I see things differently, I *understand* them."

According to Eliade, death is a component of learning. Miller's concept of ghosts enlightens understanding beyond the shadows and specters of the negative aspect of this present ambivalent existence. Miller himself conceives of a way of seeing which not only incorporates unconscious images, but gives them a powerful place in the academic endeavors of the future. In the introduction to *Hells and Holy Ghosts,* Miller writes:

"This book's project is a therapy of ideas - Christian ideas. It is a quest for images lurking in those ideas like specters, unconscious images, which, if religiously positive, are also and at the same time, humanly negative. There is here a presupposition that images of deep human significance are 'fundamentally ambivalent'..."

There is a fundamental ambivalence found in any partnership of myth with another academic discipline. This mutual conflict of feelings introduced by images and their trappings in myth both contains and consumes immense stores of spiritual, emotional and mental energy. This fact is testified to by the long life which mythology enjoys, compared to psychology, sociology, physiology, and numerous other academic disciplines. 'Ologies' come and go, but stories live on, providing vital conduits between human activity and the meaning of existence. Although myth gives clues to the history of our ancestors, it cuts through the bonds of linear time to invite each generation to investigate the ultimate questions of life, encouraging the creation of new images to tell its own story from a different perspective. In other words, history serves myth. Even if taken from a cyclic understanding, the Western style of dividing time into past, present, and future describes only one way of dealing with time. Historical facts about Clare and her times will weave through this dissertation, but not in a chronological order. Flowing through the topics, time will be present in what Marie von Franz describes in her book *Psyche and Matter* as, "one of the great archetypal experiences of man," which "has eluded all our attempts toward a completely rational explanation." So it is with myth. It hides in the mists and shades, the shadows and intuitions of that which defies definition and explanation. As with time, myth simply "marches on."

Logic partners not only word, but also image. Myth and literature are keepers of the image in their propensity to "see through" as one "looks at" a symbolic rendition of an experience. Like groping in the dark and awaiting the interchange of thought and touch, the ghosts of myth and poetry forge a way which sees through the darkness. They constitute a creatively ingenious mode of joining the poet to the mythologist in a style of storytelling passed down through the ages in written and oral traditions.

It is clear that mythology penetrates a diversity of academic disciplines. However, taken by itself, is mythology a viable lens through which to observe and interact with the world, on a par with the academic disciplines of philosophy, psychology, archaeology, theology, and sociology? Can it be estimated to be an equal in humankind's search for truth through academic studies? Inclusivity constitutes its nature.

The story is a piece of the mythical puzzle, as described in a previous section of this paper. Miller adds mythopoesis as another player in the game of learning.

Mythopoesis ventures on to the field of academics as the only player who expands the game to include spectators as active participants within the essential element comprising it, the story. These spectators are unpredictable, developing rules as they go along. Flexibility and open-minded dialogue comprise the training. Most importantly, rules bend and assumptions drop, in order to accommodate the diverse modes of living through the answers to questions of the value and meaning of the game itself. No doubt mythology's presence may unsettle the established thought processes of long time players. The rule that "This is not the way we do it," does not apply.

Diverse academic disciplines travel as companions in the odyssey of this dissertation. Mythopoetical thinking and depth psychology branch off from the trunk of mythology. Efforts at departmentalizing academic disciplines would not serve the purpose of this study. However, viewing the project as a game demanding close teamwork among the players fits the intent and scope of this written endeavor. That said, it is also of import to articulate clearly that *mytho-logic* describes the lead player. Like the quarterback in football, it starts the play and determines the receiver who will carry the ball to the goal. In this context mythopoesis moves to the receiver position along with psycho-mythology, depth psychology and Franciscan spirituality. But what does *mytho-logic* look like?

Mytho-Logic: A Moronic Oxymoron?
Logic, as the study of the principles of reasoning, comes from the Greek logos, *signifying* speech and reason; reason from the Latin *ratio*, connoting judgment, calculation. Where do logos and mythos meet? Does not the study of the principles of reasoning as applied to myth

constitute an oxymoron, the unpredictable meanderings of mythology teaming with the predicated principles of logic? In high school teasings, the word *moron* playfully described someone who is "more on than off." Perhaps this combination of apparent opposites is one example of such. On the one hand, as a dance partner with empirical science taking the lead, myth remains the ever adjustable follower. On the other hand, there is another way of tripping into the light fantastic where the worlds of intuition and thought can merge.

Wolfgang Giegerich's labor of love which birthed a text entitled *The Soul's Logical Life* struggles with Jung's Notion of Soul, believing it to be the one underlying concept in all of Jung's entire intellectual pursuit. Defining and redefining accepted philosophical and psychological principles, Giegerich acknowledges Jung to be "the thinker of soul," whose thinking is on a "higher level of reflection" than that of Hegel, Nietzsche, or comparable geniuses. Not limiting thinking to be a function among the types posited by Jung, Giegerich expands its horizons by stating:

"Similarly, the meaning of thinking is not exhausted by the capacity of discursive reasoning and the literal employment of the intellect or intellectual operations. Thinking has to do with having been reached by and being committed by one thought..."

Giegerich speculates that not only does the thinker think, but the thought thinks the thinker. Is the speculation a moronic oxymoron or a revisioning of the old myth of thinking as being only discursive? In the estimation of Spiegelman and the estimation of Jung himself, psychology is science rather than art. However, Giegerich explicates his own theory using Hegel's propositions of implicit and explicit thought. Giegerich envisions Jung as an "implicit thinker" who experienced an implicit mode of thought reception through intuition rather than by deliberation. If this is the case, then intuition with its accompanying manifestations through reverie, imagination, symbol, archetype, and story can lead the dance with the help of the rational intellect which "creates" rather than only "sorts out." Myth is the music and the director of the action. They mix in the dance, not as science *or* art, but science *and* art.

How do Giegerich's ideas apply to the present study of Clare of Assisi? Most prominently, in his emphasis on "intuited thought," Giegerich struggles to articulate principles which the pure empiricists (if there be such) may find absurd. He ventures into the muddy waters of that which cannot be empirically proven and uncovers a way of seeing which he calls "sublation," that is seeing the whole meaning of the story within its particular main events; the whole is in its parts. In Chapter 6, Giegerich models his method by applying it to the myth of Actaeon. I will piece together a myth of a Clare "in absentia," a Clare present in the spaces and omissions within her few extant writings. This endeavor differs from that of Giegerich in that the hagiographical story serves as a starter, however the myth will evolve in the process of writing this paper. Giegerich serves as a reference point for tracing a soul in pursuit of itself, then articulating a myth of the person who embodies that soul. What is the notion of soul portrayed in the extant writings of Clare of Assisi? Giegerich's theories which build upon Jung's "notion of soul," may aid in articulating the myth of a woman whose last words on earth were directed to her own soul:

"'Go in peace, because you have a good escort. The One who created you has infused the Holy Spirit in you and then guarded you as a mother does her littlest child.' One sister, Anastasia, when she asked the lady to whom she was speaking and saying these words, was told by the lady: 'I am speaking to my blessed soul.'" (*Pro* 162)

The Soul of this Study

The chapters in this dissertation will be organized into snippets narrating some historic events in Clare's life, and commenting on these events from the perspective of depth psychology's understanding of myth, and revisioned into a fresh look at a woman who is shrouded in eight hundred years of absence; shadow wrapped in hagiography and the canonization process. Clare's shadow *is* light, that is to say, she is a woman who is portrayed as so extraordinarily virtuous that, in the words of modern-day parlance, she has become "so heavenly that she is of no earthly good." Where is Clare of Assisi in this sainted being? Can women and men identity with her? Clare of Assisi's message remains in the tomb, although her body was exhumed, found incorrupt, and put on display in 1893. She hints at struggles within the text of the Rule written by her. The letters to Agnes of Prague, daughter of the King of Bohemia who entered the monastery of Poor Ladies in Prague in 1236, identify areas of life which Clare found important. Between the lines of her extant writing lie the little termites which ate at the peace and solidarity of her community of women at San Damiano. Her admonitions demonstrate that the termites would be named and dealt with, much like the uncovering of shadow activity in the conscious life of an individual. In revisioning Clare, it is necessary to see her from a "this world" perspective, placing light on the demons that haunted her. Although it seems an impossible task to exhume the emotions of a woman who lived eight hundred years ago, living evidence remains in the persons of the women who follow her way to this day. She exerts a power strong enough to inspire a present-day nun like Sister Mary Colette of the Immaculate Heart of Mary. This member of the Santa Barbara Poor Clare Community, smiles out from a photo printed for her funeral card where she is quoted as saying, "I am so happy to be a Poor Clare." Clare can be and is made known to the twenty-first century human being.

Present and past literary works, in addition to gods and goddesses, play parts in finding Clare of Assisi alive and well. Specific myths from the Graeco/Roman mythology literary works and legends illuminate aspects of Clare's personality and story, and will help form the loom upon which to develop a whole from bits and pieces. The chapters will weave a topical tapestry whose colors and threads represent elements of the human condition: love, loneliness, affection, relationship, community, femininity, contemplation, and spirituality. This topical approach will include historical events, but not necessarily in chronological order. The historical settings will be like a skeleton upon which the flesh of Clare's human reality will be molded.

Enter Depth Psychology

Depth psychology enters the stage with its cast of characters: shadow, archetype, transcendent function, soul, and a chorus of complex voices. Will eight-hundred-year-old manuscripts sustain the gaze of a twenty-first century psychological scrutiny? Will this study of Clare disintegrate into another attempt to analyze the past through the lens of the present and thereby dissolve into a roll of yarns more tangled than the original hagiographical story? Perhaps.

There is the risk that Clare's myth can be corrupted as described by Adolf Guggenbuhl-Craig in the text *The Old Fool and the Corruption of Myth*. In pointing out the psychopathologies within commonly held beliefs, such as the notion that an old man and woman be necessarily wise, Guggenbuhl-Craig expresses suspicion concerning "self-evident truths," such as the commonly accepted myths of equality among people, modern notions of progress, and the unreality of democracy, to name a few. He states:

"It is the belief of our so-called scientific age that natural sciences can shed light on psychological matters, politics, economics, literature, and history. The era of this belief is coming to an end. A new idea is spreading, that everything psychological - whether it concerns an individual or societies - can only be portrayed in images, stories, and rituals. This is my conviction. ... It is therefore essential that we recognize the nature of myths - their curses as well as their blessings - in this post scientific and neo mythic age."

Will this effort end in a tale conjured by an old fool who wants nothing more than to live, let live, and enjoy the process? Possibly. I question the conviction of Guggenbul-Craig that the all that is psychology can only be portrayed in images, stories, and rituals. It is not within the scope of this dissertation to pursue that issue. However, it is also my belief that myths must be taken with a grain of suspicion, a glob of reflection, and a plate full of playfulness.

Part II

Chapter Three
Clare's Face of Love

The "Eros" Arrow

> Set me like a seal on your heart, like a seal
>   on your arm;
> For love is stronger than death, jealousy
>   (devotion) relentless as Sheol.
> The flash of it is a flash of fire, a
>   flame of Yahweh's Self.
> Love no flood can quench, no torrents
>   drown.

(The Song of Songs 8: 6-7a)

Clare of Assisi often employs the book of the Bible named "The Song of Songs," also known as the "Canticle of Canticles," or "Song of Solomon," to describe her love relationship with God. It could be said that love defines Clare's being. The word *love* has been interpreted, romanticized, defined, described, and passionately reiterated throughout time. Clare of Assisi passionately clung to this ever-elusive love as the overwhelming purpose for her being and the cause of all created life: to love and be loved. This ever-elusive phenomenon needs further consideration, albeit short in scope and limited by yet another effort at articulation.

The word *love*, in the language of the American English verb form, means: 1. To feel love for. 2. To like enthusiastically. The object of the love is inferred and not contained within the word itself. In some other languages, such as Arabic, the quality or tenor of a relationship is understood by using a different word to name that connection between persons. The love between a husband and wife is not the same as that between son and mother, mother and daughter, friend and friend, the human and the divine, and on into the immense diversity of relationships which imply that there is care, affection, and particularity within its scope of meaning. Why is this important to the question of the relationship in regard to Clare?

Love is a puzzle of many pieces, its final picture unknown. Only the size and shape of each piece gives evidence of the right connection to the whole. The final scene is always in progress, not predetermined by the lovers. No person's puzzle is identical because love's form is unique to each human being. As diverse as the features in a human face, its variety cannot be narrowed to any one particular manifestation. Every face has eyes, nose, mouth, cheeks, jaw and a singular bone structure. Love has service, care, sacrifice, loyalty, and presence with freedom as its structural features. Evasive as a wraith in a dark woods, love cannot be concretized and stabilized. It brooks no interference in its attracting power. Once experienced, love inhabits mind and memory as welcome or unwelcome tenant. Love scorns objectivity. Blind and deaf, love swoops on her prey like an eagle, forgetting self in the desire to become one with the object of its longing.

It is the beginning and the end. When all else has been written and spoken, it is the only syllable remaining with a life of its own, accountable to no one.

C. G. Jung, in the section added to the end of his autobiography and entitled "Late Thoughts," admits to the pervasive yet always evasive quality of love. He is moved to point out that there is a force field equal to that of the power of reflection, "…in which rational understanding and rational modes of representation find scarcely anything they are able to grasp. This is the realm of Eros" (*Memories, Dreams, Reflections*). In a few pages, Jung describes what he considers "the highest and the lowest, the remotest and nearest, the greatest and the smallest." It seems that all the oppositional duality is embedded in the love of which he speaks. Jung ends the chapter by saying:

"For we are in the deepest sense the victims and the instruments of cosmogonic 'love'. I put the word in quotation marks to indicate that I do not use it in its connotations of desiring, preferring, favoring, wishing, and similar feelings, but as something superior to the individual, a unified and undivided whole. Being a part, man cannot grasp the whole. He is at its mercy."

Why, with its unutterability and complexity, would I attempt to encircle the next chapters of this dissertation within the hedge of love? The answer is simple. Because Clare began, continued and ended her life in love with all. Love for God permeated every pore of Clare's body and sigh of her spirit. She burned with love for God and that burning inflamed the world around her as totally as a dry forest gives itself over to the flames of a consuming fire.

From this point through the remainder of this study, compilations of translated documents researched by Franciscan scholars will be quoted and/or referred to as resources. The following list of abbreviations will be used to identify the particular work:

> *ED*: *Clare of Assisi--Early Documents*
> *F/C*: *Francis and Clare--The Complete Works*
> *Pro*: *The Acts of the Process of Canonization* 1253
> (from *ED* 125-75)
> *Test*: *Testament of Clare (*from *ED 54-59)*

R: *Rule/Form of Life* written by Clare
*(*from *ED* 60-77)
Om: *St. Francis of Assisi--Omnibus of Sources:*
Writings and Early Biographies
FS: *Francis the Saint*
FF: *Francis the Founder*
FP: *Francis the Prophet*
Cl 1: Clare's first letter to Agnes of Prague
(*ED* 33-38)
Cl 2: Clare's second letter to Agnes of Prague
(*ED* 39-42)
Cl 3: Clare's third letter to Agnes of Prague
(*ED* 43-46)
Cl 4: Clare's fourth letter to Agnes of Prague
(*ED* 47-50)

Thomas of Celano, in his first Life of St. Francis, attests to Clare's nobility and virtue. He says that "The lady Clare, a native of the city of Assisi... lived unto the advantage of many and as an example to a countless multitude. She was of noble parentage, but she was more noble by grace... a youth in age, but mature in spirit." (*Om* 244)

Clare chose love to define her existence, but the definition of that love defies articulation. It can only be observed and described. Eight hundred years of collective memory cannot be denied. Other women of history have loved God and humankind. Clare is remembered. What is unique to Clare? Looking at the features of her life in retrospect, what are its singular characteristics? Part 2, "The Features of Clare's Love," will discuss three of these characteristics.

Whatever the characteristics of her love, Clare needed an historical vessel on which her ideal could sail into future generations. By the thirteenth century, few institutions manifested the longevity of the Catholic Church. Despite its history of violence and greed, it included a mystical tradition of prayer and devotion to God which grounded Clare's faith. Although her personal love for God will not form a main topic for this dissertation, mention of this aspect of her love is basic to the truth of who she was and is yet seen to be. It is that relationship that generated the energy to found and continue the form of life at her first monastic home of San Damiano, and characterized any new foundation that followed Clare's style of embodying love. To Agnes of Prague, daughter to the King of Bohemia who desired to become a Poor Lady, Clare writes extensively on the theme of espousal in her first letter (Cl 1, *ED* 33-38). To Lady Agnes, Clare states frankly that "...You took a spouse of a more noble lineage... the Lord Jesus Christ." (*ED* 35)

Relationships of love undergird Clare's three main characteristics of her form of life: open-minded contemplation, spousal relationship to Jesus Christ, a self-knowledge and self-identity based on the reflected glory of Christ. In a fourth and last letter written in 1253, the year of Clare's death, she leaves Agnes with a glimpse into the transforming power of the love of God as she experienced it. She writes:

"When you have loved [Him], You shall be chaste; when You have touched [Him], You shall become pure: when you have accepted [Him], You shall become a virgin (from the Divine Office of the feast of St. Agnes). Whose power is stronger, Whose generosity is more abundant, Whose appearance more beautiful, Whose love more tender, Whose courtesy more gracious. In Whose embrace You are already caught up; who has adorned Your breast with precious stones and has placed priceless pearls in Your ears and has surrounded You with sparkling gems as though blossoms of springtime and place on Your head *a golden crown as a sign [to all] of your holiness"* [Italics indicates that the words are from the Divine Office of St. Agnes] (Cl 1, *F/C 191*).

The object and subject of Clare's love are embedded in a vision of a God whose being IS love, a God whose goal is that humans be happy within the unique gift of human existence. Agree or disagree with Clare, it is central to her being. It is the one aspect which remains constant as we look at the life of this extraordinary woman.

A Closer Look at Clare

Ingrid Peterson, O.S.F., author of *A Biographical Study of Clare of Assisi,* traces the life of Clare within the political, social, economic, and religious environs of her historical setting. The text follows an historical, chronological order for the most part. Caroline Bynum-Walker's research into medieval history, and that of other scholars, help Peterson to paint a picture of Clare within the environment of her times. Peterson comments that "The known details of Clare's early life in the first decade of the thirteenth century are minimal."

The following historical sketch includes information gleaned primarily from Peterson. Less extensive biographies of Clare by Sister Francis Teresa OSC (1995), Nesta de Robeck (1951), Sister Chiara Augusta Lainati OSC (1994), and Sister Mary St. Paul, PCC (2000) add some further background. *Francis of Assisi by* Arnaldo Fortini provides a personal assessment of the social environment surrounding the youth of the thirteenth-century Assisi and is particularly helpful in envisioning the importance of the mythological past of Assisi. References to original documents depend upon the translations found in *Francis and Clare--The Complete Works* (Classics of Western Spirituality Series 1982), and *Clare of Assisi - Early Documents* (1988).

Returning to the issue of the details of Clare's personal life, it is known that they swirled about in the stormy environment of the tumultuous era of a failing feudal system and an emerging merchant class. The late twelfth and first half of the thirteenth century, through which she lived, boiled in the cauldron of political and economic unrest within what is present-day Europe and the Middle East. The commune of Assisi was centrally located on a main trade route. The Crusades opened avenues of cross-cultural trade and diverse world views, which whet the appetites of the soldiers and opened their eyes, for the first time, to the wealth and culture beyond their tiny fiefdoms. A growing merchant class traversed the newly developed trade routes between cities in Europe and the Middle East. Merchants became the monied class, as the nobility slowly ebbed both in power and political influence. Emperor Frederick II and Pope Innocent III gathered armies to protect their own empires and land holdings. The feudal system, with its stratification of people into Aristocrats, Clerics, and Peasants, was disintegrating. Another stratification of humanity emerged, with the monied merchants at the top, followed by the hired laborers, followed by the farmers, using today's terms. While the political Empire of Frederick warred with the Roman Church Empire, the merchants gathered their wealth and developed a cross geographic and cross cultural network of commerce and communication. Economic and political power bases shifted from the feudal noble class to the monied merchant class.

Assisi played a primary role in the development of a new merchant class due to its strategic position on a major East-West trade route. However it remained politically unpredictable, with no clear allegiance to either the Pope or the emperor. The small commune fought to be in charge of its own affairs and its own future. Peasants and the upwardly mobile classes of citizens in Assisi targeted noble families as allies of the occupational forces of the Germanic Empire whose fortress, on the Rocha Majora, loomed menacingly over Assisi and the Umbrian Valley. Although the eventual fall of the fortress reinforced the claim of the Papacy to govern the Duchy of Spoleta, to which Assisi belonged, civil freedom remained the intent of the commoners of Assisi. Fortini, in his biography, entitled *Francis of Assisi* (1992) comments that the destruction of the Rocha heralded the fall of Assisi's feudalism.

The present Catholic historical era has much in common with that of the twelfth century. In both eras, the laity or nonclerical members of the community claimed their rights to take hold of their place in the organization of the church and the authority over their own lives. The Gospel message became involved in the affairs of the poor and working classes. However, to the credit of present-day Catholicism, the Vatican Council of 1968 ushered in an era of change without making war. It also incorporated two movements in the renewal, those of the person-oriented Charismatic Prayer Movement and the societal oriented Cursillo Movement. Both of these reenergized the faith of the lay person in the church, leading to the deep changes which transported the Catholic Church into the modern age. The laity claimed their share in the administration and spiritual ministry of the church, causing creative and agonizing conflict within the and among the community of believers. However, these conflicts did not cause bloodshed or war as in the time of Clare. This being the case, what do the early years of Clare's life look like, and how were they affected by the warring around her?

Clare's early reputation as a kind and giving person was well recognized, as described by family and friends who knew her from her youth. There were stories of a prophetic nature prefiguring her eminence in history. Bona Guelfuccio, who knew her from the time Clare was a child, testified at the Process of Canonization that "she firmly believed because of the great holiness of her life which [Clare] had before and after she entered religion, that she had been sanctified in her mother's womb." (*Pro*17.1) Concerning being blessed prior to birth, further testimony is given by Sister Cecilia, sixth witness in the canonization process. She tells the interviewers:

"…She heard from Saint Clare's mother when she was carrying this child and was standing before the cross praying that the Lord would help her in the danger of childbirth, she heard a voice that told her she would give birth to a great light which would greatly illuminate the world." (*Pro.* 152)

The Legend of St. Clare (ED 184-239) was written in 1255-56. It gives further information concerning the prefiguration of Clare being "a great light" which "would illuminate the world." In an introductory commentary on the work, Regis Armstrong discusses its uncertain authorship. Nonetheless, it is believed by scholars to give evidence of its authenticity due to its data which were gathered from personal experiences and from official church documentation. I refer to the *The Legend* within the context of this study because it describes the beginnings of

Clare in symbolic language. I do not venture to use it as an empirical study based upon factual history. Researchers are yet to determine the full significance of the legend for Franciscan scholarship. Nonetheless it offers vivid pictures to the imagination, while incorporating poignant references to Clare's birth and noble lineage. Clare inspired this composition which soars on the wings of poetic language. History may live in the mind, but humanity lives in the imagination. Thus the author calls Clare "A woman, admirable by name [Clare], -illustrious by designation and in virtue -took her origin from a lineage already sufficiently illustrious in the city of Assisi:..." About Ortulana, Clare's mother, it is said that she "... who would give birth to a fruitful plant in the garden of the Church, was herself overflowing in no small way with good fruits." The writer continues to speak of Ortulana's good works, devotion to prayer, and "beyond the sea" pilgrimages (190). Identity of purpose and destiny shine through the very names of Ortulana and Clare. Ortulana means gardener:; Clare means light. *The Legend* describes a voice which Ortulana heard before the birth of Clare:

"...*she heard a voice saying to her* (Acts 9:4) "Do not be afraid, woman, for you will give birth in safety to a light which will give light more clearly than light itself." Taught by the oracle, when the child was born,... she ordered that she be called Clare, hoping that the brightness of the promised light would in some way be fulfilled according to divine pleasure."

Clare knew the ravages of war early in her life, despite the lofty prophetic oracles. Due to the animosity of the citizenry toward the nobility, the five-year-old Clare Offreduccio became a refugee, fleeing Assisi in 1198. The aristocratic family of Faverone Offreduccio, which boasted seven knights, sought refuge in the neighboring town of Perugia, whose loyalties lay with the Papacy. Meanwhile, the people of Assisi stormed the Rocha Maggiore citadel, symbol of the oppressive influence of the Germanic occupation, and pillaged the homes of the fleeing aristocracy. The Offreduccio family returned to Assisi when Clare was nine or ten years of age. What happened in Clare's life between the years 1198 and 1208 before she is recorded to have heard Francis Bernardone's preaching at the cathedral of San Rufino? What was she like before she joined Francis?

The *Process of Canonization* records that Clare chafed at the chasm between the rich and the destitute from her youth. She worked to bridge the gap between the rich and the destitute in the years before she sharpened the focus at San Damiano. Lady Bona Guelfuccio testified that she had often stayed at the Offreduccio home and conversed with the youthful Clare. She also commented that Clare would send food from her own table to the poor, reporting that she "used to send to the poor the food she was supposed to have eaten and she, the witness, testified that many times she had brought it to them" (*Pro* 172). It appears that from an early age Clare could not stomach the fare of the nobility while others starved. Later in her life, Clare identified with Francis in believing that poverty is a way of total dependence upon an abundantly loving God, and a solid stance from which to return that love.

Others shared Clare's ideals. Women friends gathered in the Offreduccio home. It is likely that in Clare's exile, the women of Perugia also came to gather around her. Some followed her to San Damiano. These women spoke of God and their own spiritual understandings (Peterson, 1-

7). It is clear from the witnesses that their ranks included servants of the household. Clare returned from exile in Perugia after a truce made with Assisi in 1203. Clare was nine or ten years old at that time; however Peterson notes that the exact time of the Offreduccio women's homecoming remains unsure. It was not until 1210 that the nobility and merchant classes of Assisi agreed that the future of the commune lay in commerce, not in the feudal economy. Only then did true peace come to Assisi.

The Offreduccio family boasted seven knights. Faverone, Clare's father, is seldom mentioned as an active participant in the Offreduccio family affairs. He may have died before the main events in Clare's "conversion," as it is named by the Church. Confirming this assumption are the events which followed her night-time exodus from her home through a seldom used door in her home. Clare's blood sister, Beatrice, the third daughter born to the Offreduccio, followed Clare only days after her older sister's flight from home. Witnessing at the *Process of Canonization* (1253), Beatrice testified to what happened when her uncles, with no mention of Clare's father, learned of their niece's exodus from her home on Palm Sunday night. She had sold her entire inheritance and part of Beatrice's inheritance as well. The Process records the testimony which portrays Clare as a young woman of unusual courage and purpose. The document paraphrases Beatrice's description:

"...Then Saint Francis gave her the tonsure before the altar in the church of the Virgin Mary, called the Portiuncula, and then sent her to the church of San Paolo de Abbadesse.*[In footnote #81 the editor remarks that this monastery church was designated as a place of asylum, and that should any violence be used, the perpetrators would be excommunicated.]* When her relatives wanted to drag her out, Lady Clare grabbed the altar cloths and uncovered her head, showing them she was tonsured. In no way did she acquiesce, neither letting them take her from that palace nor remaining with them." (*Pro* 164)

At first glance, the relatives of Clare appear to have behaved unreasonably reactive. However, seen within the context of events that occurred surrounding Francis Bernardone's sudden and radical personal change from playboy to spiritual leader, the uncles' response was understandable. Possibly, in their estimation, their niece had run off to join a group of dispossessed and dreamy-eyed wanderers whose leader, eleven years her elder, announced an impractical message of total divestment of material possessions. In 1207, Francis had disowned his father, Pietro Bernadone, in the public square of Assisi, stripping himself naked before the Bishop and citizenry, returning his clothes to his father. Francis claimed that from that time on, he had no other father but his Father in heaven. This one-time party boy of Assisi, to whom money was provided in abundance by his merchant father, now begged for food on the streets where his voice once echoed with love songs and bawdy laughter. He had been the leader of youthful Assisians of his day. Now Francis was found begging stones to rebuild a church where he declared that Jesus spoke to him from the cross, requesting that Francis "rebuild my church." San Damiano, the first church which Francis rebuilt from stones and moneys begged in Assisi, was to become the home of his friend and her sisters, known as the Poor Ladies of Assisi.

The most dramatic occurrences of Francis Bernardone's tumultuous conversion took place in the early years of Clare's life, some of which time she lived in

Perugia. She no doubt heard of him in the town gossip before she first heard him preach in the church of San Rufino in 1208. Clare was then fifteen. What gossip might she have heard about this unpredictable Francis, who was destined to become her soul mate?

The Man in Clare's Life

Anyone who is of the Catholic tradition knows of St. Francis of Assisi. He is the "father" or founder of an order of priests, brothers, sisters, and lay people who choose to follow his interpretation of the Gospel message of Jesus Christ. His is one of the five basic Rules of Life approved by the Catholic Church as a bona fide form of living the Gospel. Even outside of the Catholic religion, Francis is honored as the patron of ecology because of his great love for animals and nature. Statues of him surrounded by birds often grace gardens. A story narrates that upon one unsuccessful attempt to speak of God's love to a group of non-receptive townspeople, Francis came upon a flock of chattering birds and asked them to be still while he told them of their creator. It is said that they did as he said.

There could be no greater difference between the early life experiences of Clare and Francis. Something of Clare's beginnings have been discussed previously. However, what may life have been for the young man, Francis, who would become her friend, advisor, and partner in founding a new style of living in freedom?

Francis Bernadone was born to Pietro and Lady Pica Bernadone in 1181 or 1182. His father belonged to the fast growing class of wealthy merchants who traveled to other countries to buy the objects of their trade; in Pietro's case, colorful and precious fabrics. The Assisi of Francis's youth offered a multitude of experiences, especially to a young man who was pampered and spoiled by his adoring father. Francis learned the rudiments of his religion in his parish school of San Nicolo (Fortini 98). He was likely taught to write and read in Latin, as were the boys of his town. No doubt, it was the travel away from Assisi, primarily in France, the homeland of his mother, which added knowledge in the ways of the commerce and the mores of other countries. Boys came into their majority at about fifteen years. Already at twelve or thirteen years of age, Francis's ambitious and enterprising father took his son on buying trips to France. He learned to speak French, which was the major language used in trade. More importantly, the stories of knightly conquest on the battlefield and in the hearts of beautiful ladies sparked the imagination of this rambunctious and charming youth. Unlike Pietro, whose love for France and its culture inspired the desire to amass wealth and land, his son imagined the fame of knighthood and nobility. Chretien de Troyes' tale, "The Story of the Grail," made the circle of royal courts in the Europe of the time. Wolfram Von Eschenbach (1195-1225), in his *Parzival*, the story of a young man seeking fame and knighthood, moved de Troyes a step further into the medieval dream of an honorable feudal system telling tales of kings and knights, love and war, palaces and battlefields, honor and adventure. Youthful Francis burned with the desire to become a great knight himself, perhaps after the model of Parzival.

Thomas of Celano portrays Francis as a youth of grandiosity in all manner of living. Early in life, Francis made the most of the entertainments available to him and his companions of Assisi. It is reported by his biographers that he led a gang of young men who caroused through the streets of Assisi, inebriated with wine and singing troubadour's songs of love and conquest. Brother Thomas of Celano, who died in 1260, describes the environment and upbringing of the youth of Assisi. In a biography entitled *The First Life of St. Francis,* written in 1229, just three years after Francis's death, Celano writes:

"...From the earliest years of his life his parents reared him to arrogance in accordance with the vanity of the age. And by long imitating their worthless life and character he himself was made more vain and arrogant.

A most wicked custom has been so thoroughly ingrained among those regarded as Christians, and this pernicious teaching has been so universally affirmed and prescribed, as though by public law, that, as a result they are eager to bring up their children from the very cradle too indulgently and carelessly...

But when they begin to enter the gates of adolescence, what sort of individuals do you imagine they become?"

(Armstrong, Hellman, and Short, *FS* 182)

Arnaldo Fortini elaborates on Celano's critique of the "wicked customs" prevalent at the time, by giving a picture of one celebration known as The Feast of Fools, which Fortini calls "uproarious and licentious." On December 26th, the boys would choose one from among their group to act as "bishop for the day." He was dressed in clerical robes and led to the church where he presided over a Mass. The original purpose of this event was to be a reminder to those in authority that they were to serve and not lord it over the populous. It was to teach humility. However, according to Fortini, Francis came of age during a time of moral abandon. Fortini describes orgies in which "Lewd priests, libertine men, and half dressed women joined the youths" (99). Carts carrying women bound hand and foot were driven through the city, the women being sold in auction to the highest bidders. According to the chroniclers referenced by Fortini, the song "Duc Tau, Adam" would be sung in the streets of Assisi. Translated it proclaims, "From Paradise's beautiful hall I was thrown out because of a girl who shone like a star. Do not believe a woman! Free yourselves, free yourselves! Do not believe a woman."

How paradoxical that during an era when championing a lady was an honor given a knight, the story of Adam and Eve appeared to provide an excuse for abusing women -not too different from today. That being what it may, the feast lasted until December 26th or 28th (biographers differ), when the youth-bishop would be taken in procession to the home of the Bishop. There the Bishop was asked for an accounting of his stewardship and expected to answer the questions of the young stand-in. There would be more eating and drinking followed by a blessing, ending the celebration. It would be difficult to believe that Francis was not part of these festivities which extended over a month's time, if for no other reason than to save face with his companions.

Julien Green, in his biography, *God's Fool - The Life and Times of Francis of Assisi,* takes exception at downplaying the dissolute behaviors open to a youth of Assisi in Francis's time, and suggests that his biographers cover the reality in generalizations. He comments:

"...Francis was brought up in a whirlwind of pleasures. And it is here that his biographers grope for the most respectable words to speak the truth without actually speaking it. Generations have handed down the word *farandoles*; Francis's misconduct was limited to dancing the farandole - and so the biographers dance around the truth."

Green continues to clarify by quoting some of

Celano's descriptions concerning a Francis in his early twenties, some of which read:

"...More advanced in frivolity than all his comrades ...In other respects an exquisite youth, he attracted to himself a whole retinue of young people addicted to evil and accustomed to vice. He could be seen flanked by his infamous band, striding forward grandly, head held high, through the public squares of Babylon."

Green holds that later biographers such as the Franciscan theologian and philosopher, Bonaventure, spiritualize Francis, camouflaging the more human aspects which would show Francis to be the sinner which he himself claimed he was in his youth, before his conversion. Fr. Damian Vorreux , O.F.M. (Order of Friars Minor), in the introduction to the English versions of Bonaventure's two lives of Francis (*Om* 618-623), offers an explanation of why the more spiritual aspects emerged in the style employed by the author. The works were commissioned by Rome to be a compendium of all other writings about Francis done before 1260. Vorreux explains that Bonaventure's biographies reworked previous writings and emphasized the soul of events rather than their chronology. Bonaventure looked to the spirit of Francis and the Order rather than a strict rendering of the historical events. Nonetheless, the historical milieu within which Francis matured was one of social upheaval, political turmoil, and behavioral erraticism. Perhaps Francis likely took an active part in some of its more flagrantly immoral aspects as judged by his own day.

Fortini's recounting of the Festival of Fools suggests two probabilities which give a further look into the Assisi of Francis and Clare. One was that the Feast itself was reminiscent of the pagan Saturnalia known as the

"December Liberties." Julien Green discusses the Feast in this 1982 biography, however with less vivid description than Fortini. Assisi was a Roman garrison where a temple to Minerva stands in the main piazza to this day. It is likely that the Roman gods and goddesses received their homage within and outside the city walls. In other words, Roman mythology was well rooted in Assisi and in her peoples. Secondly, Clare and Francis experienced a very different Assisi in their young years, sharing neither economic/societal class nor kinship of spirit. The eventual friendship between these two individuals gives truth to belief in the reality of destiny. They were the two most unlikely persons to share the later dreams which evolved into the style of gospel living known in today's Catholic tradition as Franciscan. As will be discussed in the Section of Poverty, the ideal of total divestment as a way of life was not particular to them.

The biographers of Francis emphasized that he was a man of great ambition and talent. Francis wanted to be a grand knight, and with the financial help of his father, this was a possibility. Men became knights by either being born into the nobility or by proving themselves on the battlefield. Francis longed to prove himself in battle. Sixteen-year-old Francis Bernadone was likely among the Assisi's youths who tore through the walls of the Rocha in 1198. The zestful and ambitious Francis harbored dreams of being a grand knight-warrior. This could be viewed as a striking contradiction: Francis, the son of a merchant, seeking fame in becoming a knight protector of the noble class, which he attacked as enemies. I believe it is an example of the confusion which the youth of Assisi and feudal Europe may have faced. They struggled to find where they fit in the turmoil of the times. To whom would they owe allegiance? They were not unlike the youth of any generation caught in social cataclysmic change, not unlike the American youth of the 1960s Vietnam era, caught like meat between two slices of bread, fighting against an old regime, and as yet not aware of the subtle presence of a different style of oppression opening outward from the underside of their idealism.

It was Francis's passion for knighthood which eventually spun him out into a space for personal transformation, which was ushered in by a war with the neighboring commune of Perugia, a political ally of the Papacy. Fortini traces the lengthy and volatile history of dissension between the two townships. At the battle of Collestrada in November of 1202, the Assisians were defeated. Celano is reported as recording that the battle was a slaughter without measure. "The sight of those killed on the field where the fighting took place was horrifying beyond words," writes Fortini. Bonafazio, a poet of the day, records that "the hand is not to be found with the foot nor the entrails joined to the chest; on the forehead horrible windows open out instead of eyes... In a bloody battle which decimated the youth of Assisi, Francis was taken prisoner, in hopes of receiving a fat ransom from his rich father. That was not to occur until at least a year later. Eventually Pietro was able to negotiate a release for his son, but not before his son's health was broken. Upon return to Assisi, Francis failed to recapture his former enjoyment of excessive partying and of natural beauty. Like many who have tasted the ravages of war, he would never again see life through innocent eyes. Death, mutilation, and blood baths are not forgotten.

In order to get some understanding of the deep trauma which war would have visited upon an imaginative boy who had known only the protection of wealth and luxury in the small town of Assisi, the twentieth century's wars, particularly the Korean and Vietnam, exemplify this reality. Those who returned from these wars suffered the same lack of zest for life and the same feelings of futility which are recorded of Francis. Their stories were told, graphic narrations of brutality, cruelty, and torture. The futility of war raised humanity one notch up in consciousness.

However, even in captivity, Francis retained his dreams of grandeur. His first chroniclers paint the picture of Francis's buoyant spirit among the prisoners. However, upon his return home, Francis sunk into a deep depression, unable to walk out into his beloved countryside with the same freeing pleasure that it once afforded him. Slowly he regained some semblance of energy and health, but he was never in good health after the imprisonment. Nonetheless, he endeavored to pick up with his old ways of life. But Francis had changed. Although gifted in the business field, money no longer interested him. His dreams of knighthood, however, remained in place. As confusing as it may sound, Francis was a warrior, a liberator, and a lover. One can only imagine what wars raged within his own spirit. Pondering this matter will perhaps help us to make some sense of the next phase of his pre-conversion years.

The lover in Francis appears during his return time to Assisi. Former companions recognized changes in him, but retained connections with this eccentric man who willingly paid all the bills. The story is told of one of Francis's frequent moments of mental withdrawal from the events surrounding him. A dance through the streets was in full swing. Suddenly, the dancers realized that their leader was not among them. Turning, they saw Francis in a kind of state of reflection and teased him about dreaming of his lady love, to which Francis, having come back to himself, answered, "Yes, and I shall have a wife the noblest, the richest, and the fairest lady ever seen" (Green 62). Francis, the dreamer and the lover, probably understood this comment in literal terms, but his friends saw it as the ravings of a drunk man. Perhaps the love lyrics of Jean de Brienne's *Donna, audite como*, which exalted the love of love itself, claiming that it can be attained only by a knight whose heart was pure, drove the passion into later action. At this time, Francis was yet dealing with very immediate ambitions toward knighthood.

Francis again launched out in pursuit of knighthood with his father's financial help. The infamous Crusade of 1204, launched upon the preaching of Pope Innocent III, resulted in the brutal and ignorant destruction and sack of Constantinople. Among the ranks of the crusaders were those who aimed at recapturing the city of Jerusalem. Gautier de Brienne, a respected nobleman and knight, was collecting a force heading toward Jerusalem. Francis joined them. However this venture was to be cut short when the great-hearted Francis met an impoverished knight on the road and reportedly, like the saint Martin of Tours, venerated national patron of France, gave his elegant mantle to the poor man. That night, Francis had a dream of a grand palace with all of the trappings of knighthood hanging on the walls in gleaming beauty. Celano's *First Life,* made no mention of a young woman being part of the dream. However, in the *Second Life*, written in 1244, Celano mentions the presence of "a most beautiful bride" (*Om* 365). Who is this bride? Some interpret her as Francis's beloved Lady Poverty whom, after his transformation, Francis continually described as a forgotten and despised beautiful lady, in need of a champion. Could it not just as well have been the lovely lady Clare of Assisi, either as a premonition or a reality, since Clare was reaching her own maturity at thirteen or fourteen years of age, and, according to her witnesses at the Process for Canonization. would be a prize wife for any noblemen of the day? Surely in a township like Assisi, Francis, who met the public on a daily basis in his father's shop, would have seen or heard of her. This remains conjecture, nonetheless, a possibility for the maturing and passionate Francis. One fact is, however, clearly reported. The attempt to join Gautier both literally and figuratively changed Francis's direction in life.

Francis's previous dream planted him firmly in the assurance that he would be a great knight. In spite of his literal interpretations, he never doubted his destiny after the palace dream. Upon arrival at Spoleto, a fever overcame Francis. He and a companion expected to glean information about where Gautier was assembling his army, and planned to go meet them. The fever grew worse and Francis was unable to continue the journey. That night another vision visited him. In it, he is asked what his purpose is. Francis tells of his intentions to follow Gautier. The voice then asks who could do the most for him, the servant or the lord. Francis responds, "The Lord." The voice continues to ask why Francis is seeking the servant in place of the Lord. Francis asks what he is to do and the voice directs him to go back to Assisi, "...through me your vision will have a spiritual fulfillment." (*Om* 366)

The story of Francis meets the story of Clare when according to Bona de Guelfuccio he seeks her out, having heard of her goodness. The Francis who met Clare and whom she heard in 1208 was a man who had proved his sincerity in pursuing the way of God and was winning the respect of some of the townspeople. He had followers, one of whom was Clare's own cousin, and had visited Rome, receiving oral approval of his way of life. Later he was to receive written approbation and a Cardinal Protector for the group which had grown to five thousand by the time of his death in 1226. Between 1208 and Francis's death in 1226, Clare and Francis became one in their venture to live the Gospel according to their notion of God as an extravagant lover, and poverty as the surest path to reach that God. Both chose the context of communal living. Both held out tenaciously against any social, economic, and ecclesial influence which would seek to rob them of their vision. Francis weaves his way along with other persons and events which help fill out a picture of the woman Clare. The early years of her life, and the faithful friends who surrounded her in her home tell us more of character of Clare.

A Return to Clare

Clare's spiritual maturity developed before she met Francis Bernadone. Clare's mother Ortulana, who herself made perilous pilgrimages as far as the Holy Land, influenced and guided the development of the unique personality of her daughter from an early age. Clare possessed a dynamism which drew others to follow her even within the confines of her home and before her founding of the community at San Damiano. It is noteworthy that relatives and friends of Clare followed her into San Damiano. Were she unapproachable and aloof, this would not have happened. Among those who followed her were Clare's sister Agnes who ran away from home to accompany Clare only days after Clare's own departure; Beatrice, Clare's youngest sister, who joined her in 1229, and Ortulana, sometime before 1238. Although Ortulana's death is recorded to have occurred at San Damiano in 1238, the year of her entrance into the community is unknown. Other of Clare's company include Pacifica and Bona di Guelfuccio, blood sisters who were friends of Clare while Clare was 'in the world'; Benvenuta of Perugia, third companion to enter who knew Clare from the time of the Offreduccio exile in Perugia; Filippa di Leonardo di Gislerio, a noblewoman of Perugia who also knew Clare from childhood and who entered the community four years after Clare; Amata and Balvina di Martino, nieces of Clare; Cecilia di Gaultieri Cacciaguerra of Spoleto, one of the first companions of Clare, joining three years into the founding; Christiana de Messer Cristiano de Parisse, daughter of a consul of the Commune of Assisi, and Lucia of Rome, about whom little is known but who reports that Clare, "received her into the monastery because of the love of God when she was very little" (*Pro* 156). Clare's personality attracted these women, who knew of her spiritual enthusiasm while she was "in the world." Clare did not have to beat the bushes to find others of like mind. She knew them early in her life. The fact that they wanted to be with her tells more of her personality than volumes of writings. Although it is historically recorded that her form of life expanded into fifty households in Europe during her own lifetime, her first followers are evidence of Clare's personal magnetism and winning ways. Clare's communal form of spirituality, which drew them, will be discussed in the Community section of this dissertation.

Clare's innovative talent led to the formation of a community of women within the Catholic Church of her time whose lifestyle required total divestment of material possessions. Clare forged a new mold of community into which women might pour their passionate love of God and service to the neighbor, by claiming poverty as their only possession. Building upon Francis's notion of poverty as a blessing, she created an enclosed community of women whose first aim was love. All that is in this world belonged to everyone. A sumptuously provident God had provided enough for all, according to Clare. By the year 1208, when Clare is reported to have heard Francis speak in the Cathedral of San Rufino, she already served the poor, rejected marriage (*Pro* 172), and had spiritual companions. Beatrice, Clare's sister, testifies that "after Francis heard of the fame of her (Clare's) holiness, he went many times to preach to her" (*Pro* 164). Others were sharing in this new vision which she acted upon in her youth.

There were attempts at creating viable substitutes for the economic and social structures that were in place during Clare's life. Efforts at changing the plight of the destitute found proponents in the Beguines, a loose-knit form of community for women and some men, were spread throughout Europe in Clare's time. Although not under the auspices of Rome, they exercised an independent form of life, shades of which are seen in Clare's manner of life. Small industries emerged which were later to become absorbed in the competitive market ideal. The Benedictines and Cistercians were well established as accepted Rules, but not inclusive of Clare's ideal of poverty. Members divested themselves, offering their lives in dedication to God through the community and thereby cared for by the community's pooled resources. The Waldensians and Cathars chose to remove themselves from the authority of Rome; however, their movement toward poverty reflected much of what Clare desired and lived as a young maiden in her household in Assisi. Some of those who were her friends may have been active in the poverty movements. Clare's heart was well prepared to accept the preaching of Francis, a preparation done in his absence. Beatrice, Clare's blood sister who shared Clare's childhood and life before her leaving home, witnessed that Francis sought out Clare, and that they met to discuss their thoughts and desires concerning spiritual matters which they held in common. The *Process* reports that "She (Beatrice) also said, after Saint Francis heard of the fame of her holiness, he went many times to preach to her, so that the virgin Clare acquiesced to this preaching, renounced the world and all earthly things, and went to serve God as soon as she was able" (*Pro* 164). These encounters are not authenticated as to exact date; however they probably occurred between 1208 and 1212 when Clare ran away from her home in Assisi. Clare was between fifteen and nineteen years of age; Francis, between twenty-six and thirty.

Where Clare and Francis Meet

Clare's vision met Francis's in the heart of poverty as manifested in the gospel accounts of Jesus Christ. However, the life of an itinerant preacher was not to be her way of living out her life. The Church mandated the enclosure as the prescribed mode for women religious. Clare lived twenty-seven years after the death of her beloved friend Francis, years during which she chiseled out a communal form of life and continued to embrace the ideal of poverty which was Clare's way to God in-the-flesh, lived out in her own flesh and that of the enclosed community at San Damiano.

Clare's gift to history contains an element of intuition, whose truth is not yet recognized. Its fruition is yet progressing toward fulfillment. This is a prophet's burden.

It is an example of an intuition articulated by forty-two years of faithfulness to a dream: the total gift of self to God and complete divestment of both the desire for and the holding of possessions. This dream lived Clare, who nurtured it with a life of love drawn from the One she perceived as The All.

Chapter Four
Clare's Love: A Topical Study
(A mythological view)

Eyes of Contemplation: The Gaze

One means of communication with the spiritual world is the process known as contemplation. It is an experience folded into the garment of time. The Four Letters of Clare of Assisi to Agnes of Prague, princess of Bohemia, and foundress of a community of Poor Ladies, introduce the noblewoman to Clare's own understanding and practicing of contemplation. In her third letter written in 1238, Clare writes:

Place your mind before the mirror of eternity!
Place you soul *in the brilliance of glory!*
Place your heart *in the figure of the divine substance!*
And *transform* your entire being *into the image*
of the Godhead itself through contemplation.

Clare's mode of contemplative prayer lies in careful observation of the Beloved. She advises the placing of the mind before the mirror of eternity. It is a step toward touching the Divine and coming into knowing who one is, in the fullest sense of being human. She knows that the contemplative gaze is more than a look. It is an image reflected and played back in an ongoing exchange between the human eye and that which is reflected upon its surface. The interchange is ongoing in ever deepening reflections. The look of love and the contemplation of the beloved are of one piece, woven of intertwining threads of the gaze and the mind. Body and mind are caught in the embrace of the heart and spirit. It is complete in itself. Not to be repeated, its power strengthens the bond uniting the lover to the beloved. Clare encourages Agnes to practice this form of contemplation on a daily basis, seeing it as a route to self-knowledge. In the year of her death, 1253, Clare exhorts Agnes to, "Gaze upon that mirror each day, O Queen and Spouse of Jesus Christ, and continually study your face within it." (Cl 4 *ED* 48)

Clare's four letters to Agnes are invaluable sources of insight into her form of prayer and meditation. Who is this woman who warranted Clare's careful tending? History records Agnes's birth as being in 1205, a daughter to the King of Bohemia. She refused an imperial marriage proposal from Emperor Frederick II, using her moneys for charitable works, erecting a hospital for the poor and a residence for the friars. Agnes also built a Poor Ladies' monastery which she herself entered in 1236. As a noble woman of wealth and widespread influence, she was a prize catch for the Ecclesial Empire of the Papacy or the political Empire of Frederick. On the one hand, she refused a marriage into the powerful domain of the Emperor. On the other hand, the Papacy would lose helpful financial endowments and properties, since the selling of one's possessions and the giving of proceeds directly to the poor were stipulations for becoming a Poor Lady. In other words, both Powers had much to lose in Agnes's becoming a follower of Clare's style of Gospel living.

Franciscans Gathered in Prayer, a breviary supplement to daily prayer describes the friendship between Clare and Agnes as being "warm." There is no written evidence that the two ever met face to face. Although there are only four extant letters, it is reasonable to surmise that more letters were written between 1235 and 1253, the time between the first and fourth known letters. The four communications give some glimpse into the spiritual life of the Poor Ladies at San Damiano, and Clare's nurturing of the women called to change their lives.

Contemplation is to Clare what the mandala is to Jung. In *Memories, Dreams, Reflections,* Jung calls it "...the path to the center, to individuation." Clare's movement toward holiness through contemplation can be likened to Jung's individuation path to the center. They differ in that Clare clearly regarded holiness to be her path to the center of one's love for God. The New American Heritage Dictionary says that the word *holy* derives from the Old English *kallo,* which means "uninjured, whole." Jung's psychological process of individuation requires that the person involved pass through the territories of dream, shadow, and archetypes. It aims at the person becoming, "...an in-dividual, that is a separate indivisible unity or 'whole'" (Jung "Conscious, Unconscious, and Individuation" 275; CW). Jung insists that individuation is not individualism, emphasizing that the former leads to unity with the collective wholeness, while the later remains focused upon the unique peculiarity of an individual.

Clare's use of contemplation to be one with God is akin to Jung's idea of individuation as a way into the collective. Clare's entire lifetime portrays a journey inward to the place where all meet as a whole, and that journey is made in companionship with others. The peace within the community of San Damiano depended upon each sister's willingness to know that she held within her own tenuous existence, the capability to be the worst and the best of all that is human. Only then could she understand and be compassionate with others and with the world outside of the enclosure. Contemplation was her means toward individuation and the wholeness she knew as holiness. It is the bedrock of her style of communal love because it led the sister to keep focused on the heart of her call: her relationship with Christ, others, and herself. Each one active within the enclosure depended upon the others for the basic necessities of life; abundance and deprivation was shared by all. Clare encouraged the parts to be aware of the whole as reflected in the eyes of the sisters with whom she lived. She invited her sisters to see beyond the messiness of what appeared to be useless and ugly, encouraging them to recognize the "brilliance of a glory" of which they are a part; a glory that manifested itself in a split second gaze, when time and space become one, the moment of contemplation.

The Here and Now of Contemplation's Gaze

Human emotion connects the outer and inner worlds of a human being housed in the compact envelope of skin. The outer world reflected off the surface of a human eye is more than a reflection upon itself. It is an invitation to know. But how does a human know creation? A common English translation of the Hebrew word for intercourse is "to know." Thus, Mary's perplexed response to the angel in the myth of the Annunciation: "How can this be, since I know not man?" Knowing in this sense is related to an entrance into and between lovers. The English verb "to entrance" carries the same denotation, however from the emotional and spiritual perspective. When one is entranced, one is "filled with wonder and enchantment." (*Webster*)

San Damiano housed and boarded fifty women occupied with the diverse works needed to keep such a community operating smoothly. Among the tasks was that of going out to beg food for the sisters. Those, today known as externs, Clare referred to as "the sisters serving outside the monastery" (*Pro* ftnt #61, 135). Clare encouraged them to notice the beauty of the trees, the sky, the earth, and in the enjoyment of their loveliness praise the God who created them. No downcast eyes for her sisters. They were to go through and into the world with their eyes wide open. Nature's beauty was to be recognized and enjoyed. Their eyes were to give them matter for the contemplation of the One that loved them through the realities that surrounded them. Clare called her sisters consciously to be engaged with the ordinary in such a way as to welcome the unexpected as friends, and to consider interruptions as invitations to new experiences. Contemplative moments wove themselves throughout a day. Therefore, the times when the sisters were "jarred" offered opportunities for contemplation to sneak through the cracks of a too rigid life.

Charles Asher, in the booklet entitled *The Contemplative Self - the Spiritual Journey and Therapeutic Work*, offers reflections on the experience of contemplation. He emphasizes the pertinence of the art of contemplation to the work of a therapist. Referring to the "contemplative self" and "the contemplative moment" as integral to the life of a monk, Asher expands its influence into the work of therapists and the world of each individual. Asher believes:

"The experience of contemplation is archetypal. It is the attentive pause at the heart of human life, a gazing upon what is immediately given, even if that be "the end of all things... the contemplative dimension of the monk or the hermit is alien to no person. And you never know when a contemplative moment may appear..."

Clare encouraged her sisters to gaze at the world around them because, as Asher points out, the contemplative shows itself suddenly present without provocation. The IMAX presentation entitled *The Human Body* presents a bold depiction of such an ordinary contemplative moment. In the domed theater with its oval embrace around an audience of five hundred people, an image of a woman under the blue waters of a swimming pool, holds her baby out in front of her, child and mother facing each other. The two look into one another's eyes. The mother and the child are caught in the gaze. It communicates their sense of wonder, but also their open respectful exchange. For that brief interlude, clock time does not exist. The mind rests in the simple gaze and meets where measured time is insignificant. Without intrusion, the two meet as one for that moment. The image overhead disappears, but its residue remains in the silence of the theater. The audience participated in an act of contemplation. The mother's and child's gaze remains a singular experience unique to their moment of union; the sense of wonder follows.

The Contemplative "I" Has It

The human eye is the mirror of the world and the reflector between persons. As a hospice chaplain, I visit patients regularly and accompany them to the door of death. Contemplative moments spring unexpectedly from the discussions and issues surrounding the imminence of death. One patient, whom I will call Martin, having been an army air force fighter pilot and later in life a successful journalist, had little use for any matter that was not factual and rational. In its early stages, he was able to keep his cancer in check by healthy eating, taking vitamins, and living a balanced lifestyle. However as time went on, Martin found that he succumbed to pain and minor illnesses. He was unable to snap back from a fall he had, a fall not unlike previous small tumbles. True, he was getting older, but it was muscle weakness which now made him more bed bound.

When I met Martin, we would chat about world events and the frustrating complexities of human behavior. Trust built between us, and friendship ensued. During one visit, when Martin described his last trip to the emergency room after an attack of pain worse than any he had ever experienced in his life, he shared that, "It was like an alligator ripping apart my insides." I queried, "An alligator?" After which he explained how much he feared and hated alligators. "They are vicious and tear their victims apart. They're sneaky and attack unexpectedly. They're ugly, cold blooded, and merciless." I waited, then responded, "Like cancer." "Yah," Martin concurred. The wide clear blue eyes that met mine in a moment of shared awareness, assured me that we met in a place beyond the literal; a new place to where we could journey together. We spent some time connecting with the alligator, paralleling it to the sneakiness of cancer and its irascible appetite for killing and taking over the space of healthy cells. Martin began to respond in a more teasing fashion as we studied this creature. He belly-laughed over a toy I gave him of the Alligator Man of Australia, who is noted for his knowledge, affection, and respect for alligators. The toy had a button which made the figure announce "Isn't she lovely," as the man lies on his belly, face to face with a baby alligator. Martin laughed, "I'm going to stay away from waters where alligators live!" The fear began to dissipate. Sometime later, Martin spoke of his respect for lions. We moved to the open savannah and from there eventually moved into the house with his beloved cat,

Rocky.

Martin is a contented man, more able to courageously face the progressive claim that cancer has on his body. Nine months after we met, Martin commented on how strange it is that he wakes up at night and is amazed by how he has endured the very things that seemed unbearable at one time in his life: pain and being penned up in a tiny utility apartment nearly bedridden. He wondered how he did it. I realized it to be a moment when his soul was speaking. I asked if he had come to some insight about the wonder. Silently reflecting for a time, he suddenly turned toward me and again, with that deeper than a glance gaze, he quietly answered, "It's a miraculous mystery." Martin, not being a man to indulge in religious talk, remained silent after these words. So did I. We met where words are superfluous. We met in a contemplative moment.

Life in all its sickness, ugliness, beauty, and grace embodies Clare's love and is the realm of her spirituality. She chose to reach through the fog and broken glass of the surface of outward appearances. Her contemplative gaze penetrates matter in a shared acceptance of the underlying energy within the present moment. Blood and body, whether that of a rotting leper or that of an ill sister, fell into the moment of contemplation. No ugliness was a stranger to her love. No beauty foreign. Clare was reported to have cared for the sick sister personally, and she likely tended the lepers along with the brothers before her forced enclosure in 1215. Through these experiences and her dedication to her Beloved, differences became insignificant. Contemplation of her Beloved drew her to a place where the separation of sinner from saint, fear from courage, inside from outside, and violence from tenderness vaporized. She came to an understanding and a union with creation. A contemporary of Clare's, the Sufi scholar and poet Jelaluddin Rumi (1207-1273) gives expression to the effects of this phenomenon. The last verse of the poem "Sheba's Throne" which appears among the selections included in Coleman Barks' translation of Rumi's poetry entitled *The Essential Rumi,* speaks of how union overwhelms duality:

"When you see the splendor of union, the attractions of duality seem poignant and lovely, but much less interesting."

When the Gaze Hurts the "I"

What is the collective, universal aspect of contemplative love? Is there an archetypal image which is playing in the garden of Clare's contemplation? C. S. Lewis, in his retelling of the age-old story of Cupid and Psyche, *Till We Have Faces,* hides the face of Psyche in the interwoven histories of two sisters, one ugly in physical appearance and the other of extraordinary beauty. Queen Orual of the ugly face complains to the gods of what she considered unfair treatment concerning their dealings with her. After the complaint, she awaits judgment. Orual, reflecting upon what the gods said to her, wonders, "Do the gods flow in and out of us as they flow in and out of each other?" Further in her considerations Orual thinks on the idea of Socrates that "...true wisdom is the skill and practice of death."

At this juncture, it is important to note that although Clare practiced within the parameters of a monotheistic tradition, mythical motifs wove patterns in her personality which is reminiscent of universal mythemes. As previously noted, it is a challenge to see an historical figure from a mythological point of view. It is the intent of this document to be true to the character of the goddesses as pictured in their particular myths. To "mix and match" myths or my themes would not serve the purpose of mythology. I choose to move with Clare much as Lewis did with Orual, who is portrayed as walking the halls of human history, dealing with the ambiguities and messes of everyday human concerns.

Clare inhabited human history. Among the possible starting places for presenting her as a unique person, I choose to describe the features of Clare's face of love, by showing how she manifested the gods and goddesses in her words and behaviors; each emanation true to a particular goddess.

Does mythology offer enlightenment on the topic of the contemplative gaze? I believe the contemplative gaze leads beyond itself and has been with humanity from the beginning of consciousness. Scholars from a diversity of intellectual and spiritual disciplines have described the experience and suggested methods for assessing contemplation's contribution to the gift of human wholeness. It may be placed in the back of the memory, but once experienced, contemplation cannot be denied without some loss of personal integrity. The myth of *Amor and Psyche* gives some indication of the perils incumbent upon one who chooses to gaze rather than graze through life. Psyche's harrowing adventures began when she gazed into the face of divine beauty, stricken by its unimaginable loveliness. She suffers from the painful ache to reclaim that beauty forever; a beauty which could well die under the blows of the goddess of beauty herself, the divinely attractive Venus/Aphrodite.

The Curious, the Cruel, and the Costly

An analysis of the myth of Psyche and Amor (also known as Eros/Cupid) exemplifies archetypal parallels which best characterize Clare of Assisi's human hunger for the beauty of her Beloved "Whose beauty the sun and moon admire..." (CL3 *ED* 45). Challenges accompany the ecstasy of the careful gaze of contemplation. Psyche and Clare journey courageously toward the place of union with the object of beauty, a journey open to both man and woman because it is a pilgrimage of the soul. It is significant that Psyche means "soul" in the Greek. Albeit that Psyche is a feminine image, the challenge of venturing to seek and find beauty belongs to both sexes. Christine Downing, in her text *Women's Mysteries,* talks about the need for psychology to become more open to an attitude of receptivity. She reflects upon Otto Rank's call to us to think "beyond psychology, that is to say, beyond a psychology which is based on patriarchal control." This mode of thinking emphasizes the differences between the sexes in a dualistic opposition to one another, thus blocking the possibility of growth through union rather than control through separation. Downing seeks a new psychology of women which, in her estimation, "would ...move not only to a new understanding of the human and of our interdependence with one another - but beyond that to our interdependence with all that lives. And if it is true that separation is a less intense need for women, we may not need to insist as much as men   have on the separation of psyche from body or the human from the natural."

I believe that Clare encouraged one more degree of non-separation as suggested by Downing; that of no separation of the natural from the divine. She invokes her sisters to see the beauty of nature not as a distraction from the divine, but as one manifestation of the divine. The event of Psyche's acceptance into the Olympian family, suggests that the human contains the propensity to penetrate the divine. As for the experience being shared by man and woman, it is like that of "falling in love." The search for the beautiful Beloved trips one over the edge of the already known, into a free fall through the abyss of uncertainty. Woman and man share the perplexity and excitement of that fall. A Romeo or Juliet will give life and limb for that love with the same staunch energy and passion that drove Odysseus onward to his homeland. It is its own heroic journey. Even in its unhealthy and partial manifestations, love's charm draws and enchants by its beauty.

The myth of Psyche and Amor was first written in Latin by Lucius Apuleius Platonicus circa 125 C.E. Since then, the myth has played itself out in countless literary works. The theme of love found, love lost, and love imagined eternal, lives on in the writings of William Shakespeare and into the re-envisioned story of Amor and Eros in *Til We Have Faces* by C. S. Lewis. Music, from Country Western to Grand Opera, sings of the tragedy and joy of love. It is necessary that I choose one from among the many renditions of the story of love between Amor and Psyche in order to follow the flow of the goddess Psyche through the running stream of Clare's life. Following is a paraphrasing of the myth as presented by Thomas Bulfinch (1796-1867) in Chapter 11 of *Bulfinch's Mythology*.

Psyche, the third born daughter of a king and queen, is beautiful beyond compare. Her sisters are pretty, but no match for the stunning Psyche. Visitors from far and near travel to her town just for a glimpse of her. Eventually she becomes the center of people's admiration, stealing advocates from the goddess of   beauty, Venus.

The Goddess, not to be rivaled by a mere mortal, orders her son Eros to send an arrow of love through the maiden's heart, the object of which is to be the ugliest, most unsavory man on earth. However, Eros, while pouring the waters of bitterness over the maiden, unwittingly awakens the sleeping Psyche, whose eyes fly open and startle the invisible Cupid as he stares into her beautiful eyes, causing him to prick himself with his own arrow. Thereupon, Cupid tries to undo the curse of the bitter waters by pouring the waters of sweetness over all of Psyche's body, making her lovelier than before. Angry Venus vows that the maiden will have no joy from her beauty. Psyche's beauty is held in awe and no mortal man dares approach the royal couple for her hand in marriage. She longs for love and pines for human companionship.

Seeking divine help to know what to do for their daughter, the royal parents consult the Oracle of Apollo, where they learn that Psyche is destined to be the bride of no mortal man. Her husband awaits her on the mountaintop, a monster whom men nor gods can resist. Psyche accepts her destiny, goes in procession to the mountaintop, and is left there alone frozen by fear. Eros orders Zephyr to carry the frightened Psyche to a valley of flowers where she rests and regains her wits. Walking to nearby woods, Psyche comes upon a palace with golden pillars, surrounded by gardens and holding within treasures of jewels and art. She hears a voice which informs her that the voices will be her servants who will care for her every need.

Psyche's lover comes to her but only by night. When she asks to see him, he wonders that she doubts his love and says that she must never look upon his face. He asks that she love him as an equal, not as one to be adored like a god. Psyche abides by her husband's wish, nonetheless, she longs for human companionship. She persuades her husband to allow her sisters to visit her.

Against his better judgment, Eros consents, sending for the two women. When they see the good fortune of their youngest sister, instead of rejoicing with her, they become jealous. Subtly they learn of her husband's request that Psyche not look upon him. They convince her to take a lamp with oil and a knife to bed that night and learn who her monstrous sleeping partner may be. Psyche does her sisters' bidding. That night while Eros sleeps, Psyche lights the lamp to look upon his face. The beauty of the sight she beholds entrances her. Stunned, she stares until a drop of hot oil falls from the lamp on to his shoulder. Awakened, the eyes of Eros look full upon her. Then opening his wings, he flies out the window. Psyche tries to follow, but falls to the ground. Eros stops mid-flight and turning toward her says that love cannot dwell with suspicion.

The gardens and palace disappear. The worst punishment is separation from Eros forever. Sad and uncertain, Psyche returns to her sisters informing them of her misfortune. They feign regret, while in their hearts they harbor thoughts of their becoming the chosen of Eros. In the morning they go to meet their fate at the edge of the mountain, commending themselves to Zephyr to carry them to his lord. Both jump and both are dashed to pieces for their efforts.

Psyche roams the world over finally coming upon a temple of Ceres, which is neglected. Corn mingles with scattered barley, covering the floor, and farming implements lay thrown around. Psyche immediately sets to putting the place in order out of respect for the Goddess.

The Goddess appears, grateful for Psyche's service. She says that she cannot protect the maiden from the angry goddess, but suggests that Psyche surrender herself to Venus hoping to win her forgiveness and the company of her husband once again.

Psyche does as bidden, but upon her surrender is cruelly insulted, abused and punished by Venus. Meanwhile, Eros is lying ill from his own love wound within the walls of the same palace where Psyche is tormented. All the ministrations of Venus do not bring him to health. The angry Venus sets Psyche four tasks which she believes cannot be accomplished by the poor maiden. One is to sort a room full of seeds, the impossible task to be finished by the same evening. Ants come to the rescue of the hopeless Psyche and complete the job by the appointed deadline. Next, Venus commands that the golden fleece from a flock of wild and man eating rams be collected and brought back to her. The voice of swaying river reeds encourage Psyche to take heart and then instruct her how to fulfill the command. Following the sage advice of the reeds, Psyche waits until the   rams   are   asleep,   then gathers the strands of golden fleece left on the brambles and bushes. Not yet satisfied that the maiden has suffered enough for being so beautiful and curious, the Goddess sends her with an empty box into the region of the underworld ordering that she procure beauty ointment from the Queen Prosepine (Persephone). Psyche is not to open the box. The distraught Psyche, hopeless and weak, goes to the top of a tower intending to go to the world of shades with quick dispatch. However a voice from the tower stops her from jumping, and explains the manner in which she will be able to get the precious ointment. Psyche follows the directions. However, on her journey to give the ointment to Venus, Psyche's curiosity is aroused and she becomes intent on taking some of the ointment for herself, hoping that it will make her more beautiful in the eyes of her Beloved. Upon opening the box, she finds too late that instead of beauty ointment, the box holds within it a Stygian sleep. It escapes its prison and enters Psyche. She falls into the sleep of a lifeless corpse.

Eros, healed from his wound, cannot bear to be parted from Psyche any longer. He escapes the palace, goes to where she lies, gathers the sleep and places it back into the container. Psyche takes the ointment to Venus while Eros flies to Jupiter to exhort the God to raise Psyche to the status of goddess so that she may marry the divine Cupid and dwell on Mt. Olympus. Jupiter convinces Venus that making Psyche divine is in the best interests of the gods and goddesses, especially that of her son Eros. The other gods and goddesses of Mt. Olympus agree. Thus Psyche goes to dwell on Mt. Olympus where she weds Eros. The child of this union is Pleasure.

Wolfgang Giegerich, in the text *The Soul's Logical Life*, develops Jung's "notion of soul" using it to reinforce his own "notion of notion." His interpretation of myth demonstrates a psychological restatement of a given myth in terms of a conviction that its notion is totally present within each of the main events of the story. He names these events which make up the story the *determinants*, that is to say, the *moments* which hold the same truth inherent in the entire myth. It is what I would call a *contemplative* moment in which a whole truth is met in one gaze.

One moment of the contemplative gaze occurs when Psyche looks into the open eyes of Eros. Both were now aware of the drawing power of the open, unveiled gaze between them: the Beauty of Love. In their first meeting when Eros unwittingly awakened the sleeping maiden, he was yet invisible. The active power of love remained with him. Psyche became the passive recipient of the someone who loved her, not given the opportunity to return love for love. It is through the courage and curiosity of Psyche that Eros was to endure the unique pain of separation from the Beloved. The contemplation of beauty led both into the domain of Cupid, however Cupid needed Psyche to teach him that beauty is not the servant of love, but its partner. In both events, it is Eros who flees the encounter, not going beyond the act of "making love" into the realm of accepting love. But Eros finds that once beheld, beauty becomes the beholder and will not let go. He yearns for Psyche.

Psyche pleads to see the face of her lover. Eros responds that he does not want to be adored, but loved. However, the curious Psyche had to see, even if it cost her everything. In Psyche, Eros wrestles with the very love which he embodies in his godliness, and objectifies in the loveliness of Psyche. Psyche falls in love with love; Eros falls in love with Psyche. In this they are equal. The human Psyche offers three traits to the divinity; those of curiosity, courage, and faithfulness to the Beloved. Genitality is only one aspect of love making. The ongoing contemplative moments bring love's endurance when the one form of beauty dies to make room for another.

Clare's path into love was the beauty that dwelt in the body of created reality: the flesh, blood, bones, rocks, foliage, dirt, plants and sky that were to her the face of her Beloved. It is difficult to say how this happened. When Clare would join the community after an extended time of contemplative prayer, the sisters remarked that her face literally glowed with light. Her facial transformation was evident to the group. Was it at the times of contemplation that Clare entered into the gaze with fears and worries, looking and being looked upon by her Lover? Were these sorted and put into order over and over as she fought her way through the resistance of her angry uncles, the ongoing oppressive patriarchy of the Feudal Church, her "obstinate" sisters?

Like Psyche, Clare had to let go of all that is considered humanly beautiful and desirable before she found her Beloved. Once her gaze fell upon the Jesus portrayed by Francis when they met secretly for an entire year prior to 1212, she let go of all that would distract her from finding her Beloved. Clare's youngest blood sister, Beatrice, who entered the monastery in 1229, testifies that Francis heard of Clare's holiness and went to preach to her (*Pro* 164). Lady Bona Guelfuccio, who knew Clare from childhood and lived in her home before Clare ran away, is reported in the Process as accompanying Clare to the meetings with Francis. "Asked what Saint Francis said to her, she replied he always preached to her about converting to Jesus Christ" (*Pro* 172). The destiny calling Clare involved a new understanding of God as manifested in Jesus Christ. Francis and Clare shared this awakening and both fell in love with Love.

From her early years, on to her refusal of marriage, and through to the night that she ran away from home, it is clear that Clare had felt the need to give away the riches accompanying her nobility. Her own beauty lost its luster as sickness invaded her overworked and undernourished body. In San Damiano, manual labor demanded the sisters' time and energy. These women of the nobility worked at menial tasks in order to keep the household fed and clothed, donating to those poorer than they. The enclosure garden needed tending, as did the spirits of the women enclosed. They did not always meet even their own basic needs. Witness number 6 in the Process, Sister Cecilia, tells of one day when the sisters had only a half loaf of bread, "since the other half had been sent to the brothers who were staying outside." Cecilia reports that Clare instructed her to take the half loaf and cut it into fifty pieces and bring them to the sister at table. In response to her comment that this was an impossible task, Clare told her "Go and do as I have told you." According to the witness she made fifty "large and good slices" as directed and took them to the sisters (*Pro* 153). Begging for their needs, the leftovers of others became as precious to the sisters at San Damiano as Psyche's Golden Fleece gleaned from the brambles and bushes where the rams had grazed.

The descents into the underworld for Clare can only be imagined. As the ranks of her Poor Ladies increased at San Damiano, changes in the manner of living out her ideal of community and poverty were a constant challenge. The unmodeled style of communal mysticism based upon the premise that possessiveness is not necessary, demanded shifts in perspective and organization which were embodied in a smaller group consisting of women Clare knew from her early days. Women from the nobility and from the non-noble classes joined her.

Clare writes to Agnes calling her into a contemplation surrounded by the struggles inherent in communal living. What behaviors precipitated Clare's warning to her extern sisters in her Rule of 1253, where she urges the sisters to be aware of their conduct outside the monastery? In Chapter 9, "The Penance To Be Imposed on the Sisters Who Sin; The Sisters Who Serve Outside the Monastery," Clare writes:

"Let the sisters who serve outside the monastery not

linger outside unless some manifest necessity requires it... Let them not presume to repeat the gossip of the world inside the monastery. Let them be strictly bound not to repeat outside the monastery anything that was said or done within which could cause scandal.

If anyone should innocently offend in these two matters, let it be left to the prudence of the Abbess to mercifully impose a penance on her. But if a sister does this through a vicious habit, let the Abbess, with the advice of her discretes (other sisters chosen to advise and decide with the Abbess) impose a penance on her according to the nature of the fault." (*ED* 72-73)

Within the same chapter, Clare discusses the penance to be administered to sisters who are "obstinate," reminding that no penance may be given by the Abbess and her sisters out of anger. The subjects of "...occasions of trouble or scandal" arising among the sisters are to be openly addressed between the sisters concerned and once discussed, "each should generously pardon her sister every wrong she has done her" (*R*72). Peaceful calm evidently needed constant vigilance and open discussion. Clare is noted to have been a woman of "great honesty." This phrase was repeated by two separate testimonies at her canonization process (*ED* 129-134). Evidently, Clare expected the same honest and careful discretion in the sisters' use of words. The ramifications of indiscretions no doubt visited themselves upon her yet spiritually adolescent community. Contemplation and truth are cut from the same spiritual cloth. Contemplation without efforts at necessary reconciliation between persons muddies the mirror into which one gazes, be it the mirror of another human's eyes or the mirror of eternity. The holy Clare was a realist.

In Chapter 6, "Acteon and Artemis: The Pictorial

Representation of the Notion and the (Psycho-) Logical Interpretation of the Myth," Wolfgang Giegerich models the theory he presents in the preceding chapters of his book. I believe that his interpretative method can usefully be applied to the myth of Psyche and Amor. What is the notion that permeates the myth of Psyche and Amor? I believe it to be a notion of beauty. What main events of the myth give evidence of that notion of beauty as being at the base of this myth?

*Psyche, a woman whose beauty rivals that of Venus. Human adoration of Psyche's beauty.

*Venus's jealousy that an earthling usurps her glory as Goddess of Beauty.

*Eros stricken by the beauty of Psyche.

*Psyche stricken by the divine beauty of the Eros.

*Psyche stripped of earthly beauty, losing all that earthlings consider beautiful - wardrobe, palace, rich foods, art, religion, prestige, power, majestic bearing, human affection.

*The journey to the Underworld to procure the beauty ointment from Queen Proserpina/Persephone.

*Psyche fails the final task by opening the jar of beauty to take some of it for herself (reverts back to her former ideal of beauty).

*Psyche's final "beauty rest" (death).

*Eros desires his bride (Love cannot live without its beloved) Psyche, and with the approbation of the Zeus, raises Psyche to the state of the divine: beauty becomes divinely human and humanly divine.

What does the notion of beauty want the reader to know about itself, its own soul? Gathering from the events, gazing at the face of beauty may appear thus: beauty is a curse; it invites jealousy; it isolates the beautiful one; only a god can bear its power of attraction; beauty fades; personal beauty suffers at the hands of greater powers; there is no return to former beauty; beauty dies; Love raises beauty to an existence beyond itself, to Beauty itself.

Clare's life viewed in relation to the preceding analysis shows some evidence of the mythical nature of her contemplative spirit, that is to say, Psyche flowing in and out of her humanness. Clare is to be given to no man in marriage; Clare is beautiful in virtue and unattainable as a human bride; she is set aside for marriage to a god; she is placed in an isolating enclosure; she sees the face of her Lover as preached by Francis Bernadone; she becomes sick and emaciated; the church forces her to live as it demands; her dreams die; Love keeps her and her dream alive for eight hundred years. Psyche flows through the Clare who dares to break a taboo and gaze upon the divine beauty. She walks the road into the Underworld of separation from all she knew and into a yet unknown future. Like Psyche, Clare describes her own unaltered goal to attain the Beauty upon which she gazes. Clare encourages Agnes to the same focused attention, writing to her in her second letter:

"What you hold, may you always hold,
What you do, may you always do and never abandon.
But with swift pace, light step, unswerving feet,
so that even your steps stir up no dust,
may you go forward securely, joyfully, and swiftly,
on the path of prudent happiness." (Cl 2 *ED* 41)

It is an accepted tenet among writers that it is best to write from what you know; from what you yourself experience. How to write from my own experience of contemplation when the practicing has thus far in my forty years of focused attention brought me only slightly closer to understanding this strange phenomenon. Clare's descriptions and advice concerning its practice are written from the perspective of a woman struggling to explain the rationally unexplainable to those who are themselves moved by an experience of the divine which they do not understand. Clare draws us away from understanding into experiencing. However, I find her depth of contemplative gaze and perceived beauty much less intense in my personal practice of contemplation. Like Psyche, I tend to focus upon its apparently impossible demands, forgetting that there is help about; in friends, nature, my own psyche, and the universe itself. The way of my progress has been that of physical breakdowns, disillusionment with religious life, hard work mainly unappreciated by anyone but myself, beginnings of projects left for others to complete due to working myself out of a job, perceptions of being a threat to the powers that be, and frequent changes of geography and cultures. Mine is the way of the *via negativa*, if that means the way of a thirsty traveler just making it from one watering hole to next. Does this stop me from going on? No. It leads me further to see that contemplation itself has many faces with features designed for each human countenance. In other words, contemplation is meant for all who choose to follow its designs.

A spiritual intangible face, the gaze of contemplation remains just that, a gaze. The grime of life's challenges rests on the surface of the mirror upon which the gazer reflects. Clutter of a day's struggles blind the seer into a weary stare instead of a comforting gaze. Nonetheless, I find that when I skip the gazing for one day, my view of the world becomes less kind. So I go on gazing at the surface of the mirror imaged in the San Damiano cross which Clare likely contemplated, wondering when I will feel the transformation promised.

On the other hand, there are those moments in the journey when the laser beam of beauty breaks through the hum-drum, daily-ness, of living: like the distant silhouette of a tree pierced by sunbeams, the ocean's crash against a rocky cliff, the luscious laughter of a delighted human being, the smile in a friend's eyes, the kiss of the divine brushing my cheek with a cooling breeze, the smell of green, roots, and dirt. When beauty meets my soul in the matter-of-factness of nature, that is when I understand for a moment that this is the gaze of contemplation. Life takes on color again. Perhaps Clare's contemplation is not so different. Encouraging her sisters to enjoy the earth by looking out upon the beauty of the world through which they walked. Two things are sure: Clare shares our humanity; she contemplates self and nature. I believe that these led to her unique style of contemplation, free of the how-to and going straight to the who-to of the self, others, and the divine.

I hold the previously stated conjectures with some assurance. It may be thought that such an assurance would make for a no-doubt, fear-free individual. It does not. I am still visited by the fear that I cannot write this dissertation because I am not intelligent enough; I doubt that I will ever change into a level of emotionality which is above bursting out into irrational rage at a driver who cuts me off on the highway. I remain judgmental of others and downright nasty mouthed at times. This is not a confession of vices in order to cleanse my soul. It is rather a part of the mystery that engulfs me as I venture to write about a contemplation, seen as a transforming power, from the vantage point of not feeling transformed at all after many years of actively contemplating. The one great light I hold like an eternal torch, like a Clare light, along this dark way, is that of knowing that after years of disintegration, the emphasis is now with the *integration* segment of that word. This has made all the difference. I know somewhat of who I am and I like this who, with all her warts and ugliness. Perhaps contemplation has helped with that. Whatever be the case, I know I will keep on gazing and keep on writing to the end of this dissertation.

The Gaze

What fool dips into the pool of another's eyes?
Blissfully ignorant of an undercurrent
swift to ingest the unwary;
carried into the dark underworld
of liquid, molten fire.
Contemplation's shadow side!
Transforming alchemy of the soul.
Dismembering.
Dissolving.
Melting into one.

BF

The Touch of Community: Leadership

"Always be lovers of your souls and those of all your sisters. And may you always be eager to observe what you have promised the Lord." (Blessing of St. Clare, *ED 78-9*)

I am the daughter of a long-time barkeeper and liquor-store proprietor. It is in this bar in a small town in Wisconsin that I received my basic understandings of community. The whole family helped in maintaining the business, our means of livelihood. From childhood, I moved in and out of the tavern like some children run in and out of their family's ice cream parlor. Our customers were an extended family who witnessed my growing up over the eighteen years prior to my entrance into religious life. I witnessed a dad who cared for his patrons. Two prostitutes, who lived across the street and who would come to the bar for a drink with the stipulation that they would not "ply their trade in our bar," often dropped in just to talk with dad. "I'm like a father confessor and if I kept a black book I could blackmail half the city," dad would joke, then continue, "Priests should have tavern keepers teach them how to hear confessions!"

Customers who just returned from "drying out," the phrase at that time for alcoholic rehabilitation treatment, always had coffee available to them. These folks were never served alcoholic beverages. Dad cared about his patrons and their families.

I cherish one favorite family story which characterizes the personality of the bar and of its proprietor. Morning coffee and fresh bakery goods were the order of the day at Faris Bar. The story is told that one morning when my brother, Francis, failed to show up to open the bar, one of the regular customers, finding the door unlocked, took it upon himself to set up the coffee and go out on his own to pick up the rolls. Upon my brother's late arrival, he found a heap of money on the end of the bar, placed there by those who had already come and gone, heading for their jobs and workplaces. Evidently, the customers owned Faris Bar along with its proprietor, Louie.

The convent rule in the early '60s allowed sisters to visit home for five days every five years. At my first home visit, I was seated at the bar with my old friends. I was now a grown up twenty-three years of age. My brother, Francis, was tending bar. A frequent customer and friend of the family looked at me quizzically. Not himself a Catholic, I now can imagine his curiosity at seeing the once familiar Barbara shrouded in black from head to foot and sitting on a barstool, wool serge habit enveloping both the occupant and the occupied. Finally he shook his head and exclaimed, "How can you? How can you live with all women?" I flinched, not knowing what to answer. My brother saved the day with a comment that remains with me to this moment. "What do you mean?" he counter-questioned, "They can, because they're all after the same thing!"

"They are all after the same thing." I continue this section on leadership seeking to articulate that element of leadership which lived eight hundred years ago and that which existed in the community at Faris Bar. What "same thing" might they both be after? What were Clare and my dad after? Particularly, how did Clare pursue it after she left home and began a new life with other women?

Clare did not walk the spiritual path of the monk, nor that subscribed to by hermits, preachers, and social reformers. In her life previous to enclosure, she chose to live her beliefs in the context of others, gathering women into her own home and, later, drawing both men and women to San Damiano. In spite of the coercion of the Church authorities that she follow the Rule of St. Benedict, her own communal life developed as a style based upon the premise of equality within the community, of total abandonment to God, akin to the ideals promulgated by Francis of Assisi.

Margaret Carney, in her book, *The First Franciscan Woman - Clare of Assisi and Her Form of Life,* points out that the effort to bring the concept of egalitarianism into religious communal life was widespread in the thirteenth and fourteenth centuries. However, it did not endure as a common practice. Carney comments that the medieval women of the noble, merchant, and artisan classes possessed more liberty and power due to their positions in society, and often had authority over a household of servants. "The ideal mistress of such a household is portrayed as a good administrator and a wise provider for her serving men and women." Furthermore, the servant girl was seen as a model of holiness and humility. Carney continues:

"The ideal was, in a sense, an echo to the servant motif in the lives of many sainted noble women, in which the reversal of roles expected by "world values" took place. Adoption of humble behavior towards one's social inferiors became one of the hallmarks of sanctity seen in the *vitae* of many women saints. While social barriers still existed between these classes, the ideals presented in the lives of the saints bridged the gap by inculcating attitudes of humility and charity that were blind to social distinction."

Clare's communal practice of the servant motif primarily focused on an egalitarian relationship among her sisters. Centered on a personal relationship with Jesus Christ, the life was clearly explained to all who ventured to follow her. Writing in her Rule, she recommended that, "...the tenor of our life be thoroughly explained to her" (*ED* 63). Although Clare likely had strong bonds to the nobility, since women of noble families followed her to San Damiano, she insisted upon total divestment of properties and moneys before a woman could join her group. Within the confines of the enclosure, there would be equal disbursement of necessary material goods according to the personal needs of each sister and dependent upon each sister's spirit of generosity. The state of depending upon one another rested on mutual need and mutual care for one another. Basic to her sense of community was service to others, which emerged from out of her vision of the compassionate Jesus Christ.

Mutuality replaced subservience. All of the women in Clare's household were "Ladies," no matter what their economic and social status before entering her community. Sandra Schneiders, in Chapter 5 of her book entitled *Selling All* discusses the reality of mutuality over subservience in a covenantal bond of shared life (160-200). Schneiders compares masculine and feminine understandings and experiences of spirituality. She remarks on the propensity of the Church to validate the men's experience of spirituality while neglecting women's insights. Religious communities of women in the Middle Ages were not resisted; women were ignored, enclosed, and regarded as lesser humans. While the clerics feared them, women like Clare of Assisi, Theresa of Avila, Catherine of Siena, Hildegard of Bingen, and Julian of Norwich, quietly prepared the soil for a feminine spirituality which women of the twenty-first-century America are tilling and planting. Sandra Schneiders is one of these women.

Clare went further than mutuality. The prerequisite of total divestment of material possessions in order to join the Poor Ladies guaranteed the elimination of all social barriers between the women. Among the Poor Ladies, all were servants of God, of one another, and of all who came to them in need. The entire spectrum of human experience found its home in Clare as it did in the God she envisioned.

However her union with her Beloved did not stop with the negative and painful experiences of self-abnegation and suffering. It would not have been possible to attract so many others to participation in such a forbiddingly painful and insecure existence. In fact Clare was reported by her sisters to have been joyful.

Clare wrote her Form of Life (*ED* 60-77) which the Catholic Church calls her Rule, to describe the activities of the sisters and guide women who might choose to follow her in the future. It offers insights into Clare's style of mendicancy and her constant insistence upon living without possessions both personally and communally. The Form of Life clarifies why Clare could not take on the Rule of St. Benedict. But what was this rule which she so sternly refused to follow from the earliest years of her foundation, and who was Benedict?

The Touch of Benedict

The Catholic Church gives approval to written Rules set down for the religious communities who come under its jurisdiction. One of the major Rules is that of St. Benedict, who is known as the founder of Western Monasticism.

Benedict of Nursia, a Christian born in 480 C.E., was a student in Rome at a time when the Roman Empire had fallen off the brink and into the abyss of political, economic, and spiritual corruption. Overwhelmed by enemies from the north, it was crumbling under the force of repeated invasions from the outside, and a decaying moral fiber from the inside. Disheartened by the corroding culture which surrounded him, Benedict desired an atmosphere more conducive to and supportive of his spiritual call. He headed for the countryside of Subiaco, thirty miles north of Rome, in order to live the life of a hermit. His original intent gave way to a new development, as others followed him. As the numbers increased, so did the demand to develop a system of organization. Thus Benedict put his ideal into writing what is now known as the Rule of St. Benedict. The motto "Ora et Labora" (Pray and Work) forms the center around which Benedict's Rule circles. The promises of obedience, chastity, poverty, and stability of habitation establish the individual's commitment to the task of developing a communal solidarity. After almost fifteen hundred years, this monastic style and Rule of Life is practiced by over fourteen hundred communities today. So why did Clare not allow the ecclesiastical church of the thirteenth century to coerce her into accepting it as her own?

The Pope, Cardinals, and Bishops of Clare's time placed steady pressure upon her to follow the Benedictine Rule. However, Clare stolidly refused, insisting that the way of life envisioned by herself and her friend, Francis Bernadone, encouraged a unique style of living out the Gospel message based upon the premise of a mendicant rather than a monastic style of life. But what was the face of Benedictinism in the thirteenth century which may have influenced her decision not to accept it as her basic Rule of Life? Arnaldo Fortini, in his biography of Francis, entitles the section dedicated to the discussion of the thirteenth-century Feudal Benedictines as "Warrior Monks, Worldly Nuns." From Fortini's point of view, internal dysfunction was rampant in the monasteries, manifesting the need for deep changes. The Benedictines, who met the spiritually budding Francis Bernadone after he disowned his father in the town square of Assisi, treated him with disdain. The encounter occurred in 1206 before Clare came into the story, she at that time being all of thirteen years of age and properly ensconced behind the walls of her home near the church of San Rufino. It is left to conjecture whether she was present at the dramatics of Francis's final farewell to his former way of comfortable living. It is reasonable to surmise that she did hear the story of his madness through the gossip vine.

Fortini's story of Francis's public stripping and subsequent journey to Gubbio precedes the story of Francis's experience at the Benedictine monastery which was located along the route to his intended destination. Following is a summary of Fortini's story of the encounter between some of the brothers of Benedict and the freshly divested Francis.

It is 1206. In the square of Assisi Francis disowns Pietro Bernadone as his father, and returns his birthright even to the clothes on his back. He stands naked before Bishop Guido and the populace of Assisi at a public hearing demanded by his father. The bishop has thrown his own mantle over Francis and does not condemn him as a robber and ungrateful madman as Pietro, his father, had accused. The proceedings end, the Bishop exits, and the people return to their homes. The shadows of the piazza fall on the lone figure of Francis, who now has nowhere to call home.

Francis turns his face toward Gubbio intent on going to the friendly folks who live there. In the woods, close to the borderline between Assisi and a rival commune, Perugia, he is attacked by brigands and left, thrown sprawled in a ditch, bloody and beaten, clad in an overshirt to protect him from the winter cold and snow. He wanders toward the monastery of Santa Maria di Valfabbrica, which is on the road to Gubbio. The brothers there are more warriors than monks, with the gruff exterior of war worn men. They frequently entered the fray of many battles between Assisi and Perugia, possibly with motives less honorable than that of the noble knights. Francis is set to work in the kitchen, and given only a crust of bread dipped in fat. After a few days, the unwelcome guest leaves the monastery more famished and naked than when he arrived. He travels on to Gubbio where he begs clothing and food from a friend and rich man, Fredrico Spadalunga. A comrade from the days of fighting alongside Francis in the wars against Perugia, Spadalunga welcomes him, recalling Francis's courage in the heat of battle and during the time of his imprisonment in Perugia.

Thomas of Celano, in his first *Life of Francis* adds his personal comment concerning this meeting with the Benedictines. He remarks:

"Then, after some time had elapsed, when the fame of the man of God was beginning to grow and his fame spread abroad among the people, the prior of the aforementioned monastery [Celano does not name the monastery] recalled and realized how the man of God had been treated and he came to him and begged pardon for himself and for his monks out of reverence for the Savior." (*Om* 242)

The conduct of the monks would be reprehensible, even if not directed toward a "holy man." A reading of Benedict's Rule makes it clear that the monks' behavior was far off the mark of Benedict's spirit and intent. However, seen in the light of the economic, political, and social unrest of the times, the monastery of Santa Maria di Valfabbrica exemplified only one of the many throughout Europe which needed a renewal of the values and practices of their founder.

Joan Chittester O.S.B. (Order of St. Benedict), present-day author, lecturer, retreat director, and advocate for justice, was commissioned by Crossroad Publications to offer her modern day insights into Benedict's Rule, fifteen hundred years after its original writing. In her book, *The Rule of Benedict-Insights for the Ages,* Chittester reflects upon the seventy-three-chapter Rule, dividing it into short segments for reading and reflection. One section of Benedict's Rule which Chittester discusses is Chapter 53, and is entitled, "The Reception of Guests," wherein Benedict stipulates that, "Great care and concern are to be shown in receiving poor people and pilgrims, because in them more particularly Christ is received; our very awe of the rich guarantees them special respect."

What was happening in the thirteenth century that might explain the behaviors of the brothers whom Francis encountered; behaviors diametrically opposed to the spirit of their Benedictine Rule of Life? One very human explanation may be found in Benedict's division of monks into three categories. His style of life being new in the sixth century, Benedict clarified his notion of the four kinds of monastics. The four include: (1) The *cenobites* who are described as "...those who belong to a monastery, where they serve under a Rule and an abbot or prioress." (2) *Anchorites* or *hermits* who have lived through the rigors of monastery life over a time and "passed beyond the first fervor of monastic life." The way is described as one in which they "grapple single-handedly with the vices of body and mind" (33), this with the approval of their superiors. (3) The *sarabaites*, "the most detestable kind of monastic", because they have never really left the world and have become weak. They separate themselves from the law of the community and do whatever they want whenever they want, living off the best of both worlds. (4) The *gyrovagues*, who "spend their lives drifting from region to region" (34), remaining for a few days without contributing to the well-being and welfare of any community. Perhaps the brothers believed Francis to be a gyrovague. Placed within the context of the harsh realities of the day, they may have been tired of supporting people who ate their food which according to Fortini was in spare supply due to the flooding of fields by nearby Chiagio River.

However, another point of view is suggested by taking an historical perspective of the state of the monasteries. As part of the feudal system, monasteries were proprietors over huge tracts of land and overseers of the working peasants whose livelihood depended upon them. The Benedictine monasteries became formidable economic enterprises, continually purchasing land and small businesses in order to serve the monastery, and intent on keeping and expanding their domains. However, by the thirteenth century, the feudal system no longer sustained their economy and some monasteries were suffering want of food and means of sustenance.

A summary of the reasons for the corruption of the Rule and way of life is offered by Rev. Claude Peifer, O.S.B. who offers a historical glimpse into the Rule as practiced in the thirteenth century. *RB - 1980, The Rule of St. Benedict in Latin and English* is a compendium of the history and Rule. Commissioned by the Benedictine Council of Presidents of Federations, its aim was to update and interpret Benedict's Rule in the light of Vatican Council II's (1964-1968) directive to religious communities that they study and reclaim their original charism, as envisioned by their founder/ess. Under the section, 'Decline and Renewal: The RB from the Thirteenth Century to Modern Times', Peifer states:

"In the late Middle Ages both the black and white

monks fell quite rapidly into decadence. There were many causes for this, some of them external to the monasteries: the shift from feudalism to urban life ruined the economic base of the monasteries; ecclesiastical and secular princes impoverished them by exacting revenues and interfered in their internal affairs; the Black Death and the Hundred Years' War severely depopulated many houses; and the great schism of the West divided order and communities in conflicting allegiances."

It is noteworthy that it was a community of Benedictine sisters which first harbored Clare from her uncle's wrath in 1212. Likewise it is the Benedictines who gave Francis the tiny church of Mary Queen of the Angels, now known as the Portiuncula (Little Portion) which is the mother church of the Franciscan family to this day. Perhaps had Francis met the Benedictine spirit practiced in its true form, he might well have joined that community. However he was a man of his own times. His era demanded a new mode of spiritual practice to meet the changing social structures. Europe was readied for a spirituality which could be taken into its marketplaces, not away from them. Although not without much confusion, Francis eventually chose the route of preaching and mendicancy. Clare affirmed and confirmed that choice with her life.

The Touch of Mendicancy
The Franciscan mendicant order arose at a time when the Feudal System was losing its wealth and power. Simultaneously, the merchant class came to birth with its new economic and social structures.

What is clear is that Clare and Francis met at a fork in the road where each of their unique spiritualities converged into a path which is known today as Franciscan. Clare no doubt identified with Francis in his service and devotion to a God who is present in all creation. The added dimension of mendicancy exteriorized that ideal, which Clare re-envisioned and developed into a different style of implementation in an enclosed communal entity. The Catholic Tradition has kept Clare deeply hidden behind the overwhelming charismatic persona of St. Francis, therefore her genius in making mendicancy work among a community, without that community becoming a drain on the society, has to a large degree been disregarded. What did communal mendicancy look like?

The word *mendicant* derives from the Latin *mendicant* meaning "to beg." There are persons who live off the toil of others, as Benedict attested to in his scathing remarks aimed at the *sarabaites* and *gyrovagues*. Perhaps the mean spirited monks who mistreated Francis thought he was one such person. As shown in the story of the meeting with Francis, the someone accused of such vagrancy may be a victim of mistaken identity. One of the sisters with whom I live at this time, describes a woman in Los Angeles, California, who remains crouched outside the sisters' residence and is fed daily by a sister who brings her lunch. It is common knowledge that this woman receives a check monthly and is otherwise capable of paying her own way through life. Yet the sister continues to give her food and kindly companionship for a short while each day. Is the woman a *gyrovague*, a mental patient, a lonely soul, a saint? Who knows? Sister is just feeding a hungry woman, as Clare did in her day.

It is not my intent to discuss the reasons for anyone's choice or need to beg. It is more to say that the free choice of mendicancy as a way of life is uncommon and difficult to understand even in the twenty-first century. Begging is little appreciated by hard-working folk. No one wants to be relegated to pauperism, and the human response to the act of begging is no different in the twenty-first century than in the thirteenth: fear, avoidance, disgust, and judgment.

An experience of a response to a beggar remains planted in my memory. Once while awaiting the change of a traffic signal, a beggar stood on the corner holding a sign asking, "Some change for coffee?" As I opened the window to put a dollar into her hands, a car mate commented, "I never give them anything. They'll just buy a drink. I give to an organized charity." This is a practical and prudent stance, but it came from a sister who had taken the vow of poverty and whose community has needed, in its own history and likely to this day, to depend upon the generous kindness and alms given by others. Condemnation is not the object of telling this experience. Sometimes I give out of a sense of guilt for having taken a vow of poverty and then witnessing those who live it. My purpose is to show the ordinary human propensity toward looking down upon those who beg. It is to emphasize that Clare's and Francis's choice of the communal mendicant life identified them with the most despised and feared in any historical era. That they chose it for the love of God, made little difference to those who witnessed them in the early years of their transformation of spirit. This choice of mendicancy made them pariahs, more surely than their care for and companionship with the lepers. In the Middle Ages there were individuals and communities who opened lepersariums to care for the ill. There were individuals and small groups who chose the mendicant life. However, choosing mendicancy as a communal principle seeking the approbation of the ecclesiastical authorities was more than extraordinary: it was radical. Nonetheless, mendicancy formed the base of the Franciscan charism, although not as clearly practiced today in the United States as in its conception during the thirteenth century.

It was Francis who chose the route of the mendicant life. Clare's sense of generosity and the communal bond with others was established before her joining in the journey with Francis. It was her unique challenge to give birth to and nourish a practical response through an enclosed mendicant community. Francis preached in the bustle of the marketplaces; Clare preached in the quiet of the enclosure. Both begged for their sustenance and worked in manual and menial tasks to contribute to the broader community. The brothers worked in the fields or wherever they were needed. The sisters gardened, sharing their food, medicines, and healing care with the townspeople who came for their help. Written into her Form of Life is the description of the mode of existence that is to be practiced by her sisters and by herself as their Abbess. Mendicancy results from cherishing non-possessiveness as a way of life. Clare exhorts her sisters in her Rule:

"Just as I, together with my sisters, have ever been solicitous to safeguard the holy Poverty which we have promised the Lord God and blessed Francis, so too, the Abbesses who shall succeed me in office and all the sisters are bound to observe it inviolably to the end: that is to say, by not receiving or having possession or ownership either of themselves or through an intermediary, or even anything that might reasonably be called property, except as much land as necessity requires for the integrity and proper seclusion of the monastery, and this land may not be cultivated except as a garden for the needs of the sisters." (*ED* 68-69)

Jacques de Vitry (c.1170-1240), Bishop of Acre in the Holy Land and later made Bishop of Tusculum in 1228, is recognized as a reliable source for information concerning the religious movements of the thirteenth century (ED 245-256). In a letter to friends in Liege sent from Genoa, October 1216, de Vitry describes his encounter with a group called the Lesser Brothers and Lesser Sisters, one of the names for the groups gathered around Clare and Francis. After noting that the Pope and Cardinals held them in great esteem due to "...their being of one heart and one soul," as a community, De Vitry goes on to describe their daily routine of life. He portrays the brothers as engaging in active work during the day and returning to their places of contemplative solitude at night. Further in the letter, he speaks of the Lesser Sisters describing, "The women live near the cities in various hospices. They accept nothing, but live from the work of their hands. In fact, they are very much offended and disturbed because they are honored by the clergy and laity more than they deserve."

Footnote 30 describes the hospices of Clare's time as being "simple, poor houses which became the dwelling places for many of the new religious movements of women" and men. The matter of enclosure in the early years of San Damiano remains questionable. Hugolino dei Conti di Segne, lifetime friend and papal advocate for Francis and his brothers, and later as Pope Gregory IX, continued his diligent care for the brothers and sisters. In 1219 when he was Cardinal Bishop of Ostia, he wrote a Rule for the Poor Ladies which clearly prescribes that enclosure was to be practiced by the sisters. Was San Damiano a hospice from 1212 to 1219 before it became an enclosure? Were the sisters moving freely among the sick and caring for the needy alongside the brothers?

Note 30 remarks that Paul Sabatier in his *Mirror of Perfection*, published in 1898, suggests that the Poor Ladies were not originally a contemplative community but one engaged in manual and hospital work, but the note goes on to say that "The position has been thoroughly refuted" by I. Omaechevarria using the resources available in 1982. It would seem that the church had the monastic Benedictine way in mind for Clare and her sisters by 1215, and the appropriate enclosure ensued. Nonetheless, it is this writer's hope that the discovery of new manuscripts will lead present and future Clare scholars to research knowledge of the sisters' lives from the time Clare joined the brothers in 1212 through 1219, when Hugolino wrote his Rule of enclosure based upon the Rule of St. Benedict. Why did the ecclesiastics need to harness this little flock of women? Did Clare's influence with the aristocracy and the fact that the widows and daughters of nobility were joining her in unexpectedly large numbers, give the Church reason to be concerned over a tilt of power away from the church? Did the wealth of dowries in the forms of expanses of land holdings and powerful liaisons connected with these women threaten the power of these uncertain ecclesiastics? No matter what the fears and machinations of the men of the time, Clare's focused and cloistered existence went on in the midst of political intrigue, bloody crusades, crumbling economic system, and quarreling brothers. About what this community may have looked like from within, we have some knowledge. We have the Form of Life written by Clare for her enclosed, mendicant community of Lesser Sisters. In the tradition of the Catholic Church, this is the first Rule written for women by a woman which was accepted and approved in writing by the Papacy.

The Touch of San Damiano (1219-1253)

Clare offers light on the matter of activity within the enclosure, in her own rule, which she calls her Form of Life. The title of Chapter 7, "The Manner of Working," situates work within the context of Clare's vision. It does so through the use of the term *manner*. Clare considered active pursuance of a living and loving relationship with God as the Sisters' work. All of the activity of life constituted the *manner* of its fulfillment. The *Who* is of greatest import. *How* spins off from the fire and energy of relatedness to God and to life as experienced in the present moment. In contrast to the Rule of Benedict, of which twelve chapters of the total seventy-two begin with the word "How," Clare advises her sisters in procedural clarifications within a twelve-line, four-sentence text constituting the entire Chapter 7. This text also gives a glimpse into the daily existence of her sisters. (I take the liberty to insert bracketed comments for clarification within the context of the quotation.) Clare writes in her Form of Life:

"Let the sisters to whom the Lord has given the grace of working work faithfully and devotedly after the Hour of Terce at work that pertains to a virtuous life and the common good. They must do this in such a way that, while they banish idleness, the enemy of the soul, they do not extinguish the Spirit of holy prayer and devotion to which all other things of our earthly existence must contribute."

At the Chapter [general meeting of the sisters] the Abbess and her Vicaress is bound to assign the work of her hands that each should perform. Let the same be done if alms have been sent by someone for the needs of the sisters, so that a prayer may be offered for them in common. Let all such thing be distributed for the common good by the Abbess or her vicaress with the advice of the discretes [Sisters, other than the Vicaress, chosen from the ranks of the sisters to act as advisors to the abbess.]" (*ED* 70)

Begging was one of the jobs assigned to the extern sisters, that is, those sisters who were not enclosed and who moved among the people. Some of the duties of the enclosed sisters included gardening foods, both for the sisters and to be given away, sewing and needlework for the churches to use in worship, and cultivating herbs to be used in the ongoing care of the sick. These activities shaped a part of the day. However, the privilege of prayer formed the foundation and superstructure of Clare's community at San Damiano. Manual labor was intended to bolster the spirit of prayer and contemplation which was to lead to communication and closeness with God. To be and become a conscious human being in love with God composed the community's one great work.

Clare's Rule is short. It is a twelve-chapter document of seventeen pages, one and a half pages of which consists of papal pronouncement and approval, plus sixty-four lengthy footnotes by the editors. Clare's basic belief is that manual labor and kindly service are the children of love. All action finds its worth, promise, and fulfillment in focusing on the parent, not the child. If the parent, love, is honored, the children will mature healthily. Love is the work of her community's life. All else serves its purposes. Furthermore, the source of love is the God who incarnates in creation through the enfleshment of Jesus Christ. Clare's style of life does not need to negate the power and beauty of the Benedictine way of life. However, what she and her friend Francis envisioned constituted an alternative mode of living out a call to love God. Rather than choosing Benedictine monasticism, they espoused the way of the mendicant mode of living. Mendicancy distinguishes the Franciscan from the Benedictine form of life.

Clare's notion of prayer differs from Benedict's, which emphasizes prayer as being the work of God. Chapter 43 of Benedict's Rule entitled, "On Those Who Come Late to the Work of God or to Table," portrays Benedict's stance concerning the relationship between work and prayer. The phrase "Work of God," refers to The Divine Office, which is to this day the official formal prayer sanctioned by the Catholic Church prayed daily by religious communities and priests. Within its context of addressing the subject of the Divine Office, Benedict legislates on the conduct toward those who are guilty of violations against prompt attendance and careful recitation. Clare's emphasis lies in a relatedness to God which is manifested through prayer.

In Clare's Form of Life the recitation of the Divine Office is addressed. In Chapter 3, "The Divine Office and Fasting, Confession and Communion," Clare cites the custom of the Friars Minor as the model for her sisters. It was to be recited, not sung. The sisters who could not read were to recite a given number of Our Fathers for each of the hours of Office. However, ecclesiastics continued the pressure on Clare to adopt Benedict's Rule.

The hierarchy of the church struggled with the acceptance of a form of life for which Francis received oral papal approval by Innocent III in 1209. The papacy held off its full approval until a Rule be put into writing. Upon papal request, Francis, with the help of a brother, wrote a Rule in 1221, which according to St. Bonaventure was lost by the saint's vicar. Finally the Rule of 1223 was written and approved by the church. Meanwhile Clare and the community at San Damiano followed a short form of life given them by Francis and accepted by the sisters. A written text is included in Chapter 6 of Clare's Rule and reads:

"Because by divine inspiration you have made yourselves daughters and servants of the most high King, the heavenly Father, and have taken the Holy Spirit as your spouse, choosing to live according to the perfection of the holy Gospel, I resolve and promise for myself and for my brothers to have that same loving care and special solicitude for you as [I have] for them."

The church ecclesiastics continued in their efforts to convince Clare to live under the monastic Benedictine Rule, not yet aware that what Clare modeled was indeed a new form of living the Gospel. In the year 1219, Hugolino, now Pope Gregory IX, states in the prologue to his Rulewritten for the Poor Ladies:

"...we give you the *Rule of Saint Benedict* to be observed in all things which are in no way contrary to that same *Form of Life* that was given to you by us and by which you have especially chosen to live. This *Rule of Saint Benedict* is known to embody the perfection of virtue and the greatest discretion."

The misunderstanding of church authority coerced Clare into reiterating and clarifying her vision throughout her entire life. The Rule of Hugolino neglected to include Clare's concept of poverty. That of Innocent IV allowed ownership of moveable and immovable goods. Possessiveness in any form, whether in material objects or in domination over others, undermined Clare's concept of poverty as being a manifestation of total dependence upon a loving God. Her terminology gives evidence of this belief. It is noteworthy that in her Rule, Clare - refers to all of the women in her community as "sisters." Her only distinction lay between the professed and non-professed, which is to say, those who have committed themselves to make the community their primary family, and those who have not made that commitment for life. On the other hand, the Rule of Cardinal Hugolino (1219) distinguishes between the sisters and the nuns. Rendering specific directions concerning the event of a member's profession, Hugolino commands:

"If, by chance, permission is ever given to some Bishop to celebrate Mass within the enclosure for the blessing of an abbess or for consecrating some sister *as a nun* [writer's italics] or for some other reason, let him be content with as few as companions and assistants as he can." (*ED* 93)

In terms of the Church's established definition of women in convents, the women who remained within the walls of the enclosure were called nuns; those not in the enclosure were called sisters. Clare makes no such distinctions. All are sisters in her community.

The people of Assisi depended upon the sisters to intercede with God on their behalf. San Damiano and its enclosed sisters were to the surrounding countryside what the temple of Hestia was to the Greek city: a bastion of integrity where the covenant with god/esses and written legal contracts made between citizens were stored and preserved. Symbolizing these commitments was a fire continuously burning and tended by Hestia's devotees, the Vestals. At San Damiano the community also tended the fire of love for God burning continuously within the heart of each member. Holding sacred the covenant between God and the people guaranteed the sacredness of agreements made between those same people, who held to the belief that they are made to the image and likeness of God. Furthermore, with no place to call their own, the sisters proclaimed that the abode of God is not convents and monasteries, but the human heart.

The Evangelical Touch

According to recent studies in Franciscan scholarship, it has been discovered that the primary call of the Franciscan is *evangelical* in nature. The main means of passing on the message of God's love is found in living the gospel as closely as possible to that modeled by Jesus Christ, without interior or exterior coercion. Psychologically speaking today, anyone struggling to live Jung's style of the individuation process will know the constant vigilance and self-discipline demanded by such a process. To Franciscans, the word *evangelical* means that the convent and monastery live within the heart of each sister and brother no matter where they are at any given time. They become living convent and monasteries enclosing the divinity. The person becomes the home where God dwells. A standing joke among the religious communities of the twenty-first century, which humorously captures the mobility within the Franciscan call, proposes that there are only two things that the Pope does not know: (1) how much money the Jesuits have, and (2) just where all the Franciscans are.

The constriction of enclosure for Clare and her sisters seems to imply automatically that mobility belonged only to the men who followed Francis. If limited only to physical movement, it would seem so. However if understood also to mean "moving quickly from one condition to another," which the *American Heritage Dictionary* lists as a second meaning for the word *mobility*,

San Damiano housed an extraordinarily mobile community. Vested within its women was the inner freedom to adjust to rapid and unpredictable changes due to the lack of the vital necessities of existence: food, clothing, shelter, and safety. Although travel out of the confines of the enclosure was limited, there was the constant reality that the sisters possessed nothing of their own and thus lived a hand-to-mouth daily existence. Added to a flexibility of spirit and awareness of the community's basic needs was the alleviation of the poverty which surrounded them and appeared begging at their door on a daily basis. And then, of course, there is silence, which takes on its own form of mobility.

The Touch of Silent Pain

Clare's style of leadership emerged from out of the darkness of silence, a leadership which was capable of sustaining the inner realizations of one's own deepest, dirtiest, most shameful self. Can a group of women with many minds be united in order to carry on a life free of good or bad, right or wrong, you or me? Can diversity and unity cohabit? Perhaps it is in "the seeing" where communication between the Self and the other lapses. Although the eyes may be open, seeing is no guarantee, as only a blind person well knows. However, one place of seeing where brain and mind, contemplation and action may meet, is in the silent space between persons.

The concept of the space between was discussed at a conference sponsored by the Leadership Center of the University of San Diego entitled *Leadership for Change: Chaos, Complexity, Resistance... and Courage* (July, 2002). It exemplified the power and pain wrapped within the human endeavor to allow honest feelings to orchestrate the discovery of a common topic in the midst of a deeply diverse group. For an entire weekend, we seventy some participants entered with the staff into the shared task of staying with feelings which arose within the context of other member's expressed opinions, suggestions, and questions. It reminded me of the need to stay with a feeling when writing this dissertation; to write from felt experience. Pulitzer Prize winner Alice Walker, in her memoirs *The Way Forward is with a Broken Heart*, says, "What is not remembered emotionally... is not remembered." An emotionally charged experience revisits us in recalling a thought and reliving its feeling. The original experience occurs in the "spaces between" persons. In one of the conference seminars, "Too Far in Us, Too Far Out, 'Finding' and 'Losing' One's Boundaries," Earl Braxton, President of Edge Associates, a consulting and training organization that aims toward systemic change through the training of executives and managers, defines boundaries as "the space between," and further discusses that "Boundaries are what separates and defines the space between such things as self and others, what's inside of us vs. what is outside of us, and what we think vs. how we feel" (Conference Seminar Handout). Braxton explains that boundaries differentiate rather than divide, and can be instruments of unification when one knows where her/his boundary, as an individual entity, begins and ends. Braxton describes boundaries as firm and permeable or rigid and flaccid. He further suggests that they aid in helping us be able to "stay in the moment," and manifest a willingness to give up control in order to gain insight. This understanding of boundaries incorporates the challenge of joining heart to head in the same space, and the seminar continues to investigate ways and means of doing so while present in a group.

It is in what Braxton calls the "space between" that Clare shows her particular giftedness. She takes these ideas and carries them beyond the "versus," uniting self with others, inside with outside, and thinking with feeling. Her inclusion of the sisters in the decision making processes of the community was attested to in the Canonization Process. She likely experienced the difficulties and satisfactions of meeting with her sisters in the 'spaces between' and encouraged their stepping into these spaces as the main means of communication among them. The diverse economic and social backgrounds from which her sisters came no doubt made for some interesting discussion. Her leadership style was far ahead of its time in utilizing the 'space between' as a means of connection, however Clare's spaces admitted silence as a participant.

The silent spaces in dialogue and discussion can fill up with words and activities which sabotage the intent of the process. Space has the propensity to become cluttered. Thus the space between the sisters could have become an empty no-woman's land into which neither side dare venture, or it comes to be a place where a shared task and idea are discovered to the benefit of both. Clare seems to have been able to lead her sisters to the latter. She invited them to remain contemplatively present, waiting for the rigid walls to collapse, like the walls of Jericho minus its strategy of creating an external din. The internal din is sufficient to collapse inner barriers. Her quiet replaced the anxiety causing war cries of Aaron's army of the Hebrew Scriptures, because Clare's aim was to reach that inner calm which clears the way for listening. Individual stillness stands firm amidst the clamber of the surrounding environment, and the inner din of intense emotions. The space between persons is cleared for the meeting of minds and perhaps hearts, creating a climate friendly to communication and understanding. The walls between the sisters collapsed. This does not come easily to human beings, as my experience of the Leadership Conference so clearly showed.

Basically the task of the conference was to recognize an emotion which emerged in the group sharing and to remember to speak it out or hold it quietly within, rather than sift the feeling through the brain and then speak it out from the head. The group groped in the darkness of frustration, anger, fear, and insecurity as together we entered the chaos of unanswered questions and confusing sidetracks, never getting to the "it" which evaded us. We sought to discover a shared task, something we could "sink our teeth" into, like vampires needing to bleed life from others in order to believe that they themselves are truly alive. It is as if the trickster god, Hermes, were racing around the room within contradictory and tricky words that camouflaged feeling and meaning. Unidentified individual boundaries faded and rebuilt before our eyes. Now as I write this, a clear description evades me. Nonetheless, I believe that the conference brought home its message that human communication is ambiguous at least, and downright untruthful at most. This experience taught me of what Clare may have encountered by way of communication within her budding community. On the Monday following this weekend experience, I wrote:

"The Leadership Conference of July shed light on many areas of a group's power over individual peace of mind within collective gatherings. Now one day after the three day conference, I find that the strain to 'figure things out' tends to rob me of feeling the present experience of anxiety that rises when I consider my foibles, mistakes and behavioral outbursts at that conference. Everything draws me out of this present sense of anxiety and sadness that I am experiencing..."

Dualistic, oppositional relatedness where the boundaries are defined by the differences rather than by the spaces between: it is like in the heat of a battle where there is no buffer zone. There is no buffer zone, only two opposing walls with no in-between space. Persons from either side risk being killed if they move from their present position, possibly by the strayed bullet of a friend from his/her own troop. There is no space between.

Perhaps the intense emotional impact of this experience seems too personal to be helpful in a dissertational presentation. However, the fierce energy with which the participants protected themselves, gave deeper meaning to how difficult it may have been for Clare to come to agreement, much less consensus, among her sisters at their community meetings. This Conference gave me first hand evidence that the style of leadership embodied in Clare demanded an unconditional acceptance of all that one is, and all that the other appears to be. In this situation, silence is superlatively active and any spoken words come from the heart. The process demands honesty and inner stillness.

Sister Karen Karper, a Poor Clare Sister from Ohio, discusses Clare as spiritual guide. Writing in the journal *Review for Religious*, Karper emphasizes Clare's focused attention upon stillness in prayer and contemplation of Jesus Christ as the means and the end of personal and communal transformation. She encourages the practice of stillness which informs the sisters' every action without a multitude of "do's and don'ts" which rules proscribe and reiterate. What characteristics engendered her style of leadership? Can they fit into the present day mode of leading? The twenty-first century business world offers some insights into the matter.

The Touch of Leadership Vested in the Many

The entrepreneur is the twenty-first century's new economic class. The merchant class of the thirteenth century rose from the ashes of the feudal system; the entrepreneur awakens in the shadow of the impersonalization of today's big business conglomerates. Clare's style of leadership bespeaks a woman of intelligence, ingenuity, courage, and practicality. These are human qualities, the same of which abide in "entrepreneurism." They are not secret, nor are they supernatural in nature. They are human qualities lived out in their fullest potential in the arena of the business world.

In the January 2002 issue of the *Entrepreneur* magazine, Aliza Pilar Sherman, presents her study of successful entrepreneurs. Answering a question concerning who inspired each of them as models of "entrepreneurism" from the past, they offer their own description of what it takes to be a business person today. Some of the responses follow.

Michael Dell, founder of Dell Computer Corps., a company worth $31.9 billion: "Somebody who has a new idea or different idea and takes a risk and works hard to make it work."

Anita Roddick, founder of The Body Shop, with 1,800 stores in 49 countries: "Entrepreneurs are obsessive visionaries, pathological optimists, passionate storytellers and outsiders by nature."

Richard Branson, founder of Virgin Airways Ltd. and

170 spin-off companies: "An entrepreneur is somebody who is willing to go where others are not. Who doesn't often listen to accountants. Who if somebody says something is impossible, is determined to prove them wrong."

Ben and Jerry, founders of an all-natural ice cream company with 200 shops and over $230 million in sales: "Someone who has a tremendous amount of drive and is willing to sacrifice most anything to bring this business vision to fruition."

The qualities listed by these present-day entrepreneurs bear a striking resemblance to the characteristics manifested in Clare of Assisi, eight hundred years ago. Clare sacrificed wealth, nobility, prestige, family, marriage, and health to further her vision of a life dedicated to total dependence and love of the Divinity. She lived out her vision in the choice of poverty and service of the poor while she lived also as an outcast. Her forty-two years in enclosure indicates either pathology or holiness (wholeness). Clare refused to allow an overpowering clericalism to sway her off her target of developing an enclosed contemplative and mendicant community of women who were vital, vibrant, and contributing members to the larger community of humanity. These are all human characteristics pushed to their fullest potential. Furthermore, Clare manifested a unique spiritual and entrepreneurial flair for taking risks.

The Touch of Being

In her novel *Interview with the Vampire*, novelist Anne Rice reflects upon the human propensity toward needing to act, to be *doing* without an accompanying consciousness of an action's ramifications. In the story,

Vampire Louis suffers the fate of experiencing human emotions which accompany him into his vampire state. Other vampire characters intellectualize their killing behaviors and possess no feelings concerning their own cruelty and the murder of the victims. They simply "do." Throughout the tale, Louis seeks to find meaning in his existence as a vampire, reflecting upon its purpose in the larger context of life forever. The other vampires have no such need. In other words, the vampire Louis is human in his feelings and vampire in his *doings*. He is thrown into the ambiguous state of killing in order to live and hating himself because he must kill. He suffers extremely from needing to sustain his vampirehood by sucking the blood life out of human beings. Louis reflects on the suffering his awareness precipitates, and cogitates on the behaviors of those vampires who act for the sole purpose of acting describing them as, "…those people who must act. Such a person must be pushed considerably before he will open up and confess that there is method and thought to the way he lives." Symbolically speaking s/he unconsciously "sucks the life blood out of others" who are weaker than themselves, solely to satisfy their own desires and needs. This seems to be true for humans in general who seek only personal gain at the expense of others.

Conscious purpose to words and actions undergirded Clare's style of 'entrepreneurism.' Heart and intuition led head and rationalization. Rationality served compassion. Clare learned from her mistakes. Her *being* modeled her *doing*. Where Louis chose to continue to live in the state of pain, Clare moved that pain into her marriage with the Spirit of light, life and continual fertility. That is to say, she focused her attention outward toward the daylight of God and others, and wed that to her night walks through her inward brokenness, despair, and fear. I believe that, like Louis, her emotions and passions caused her suffering and pain. However, unlike Louis, Clare's joy balanced her suffering. Love sustained her. In the *Process of Canonization (ED* 125-75) witnesses commented on her honesty and joy. Negative behaviors and emotions were not mentioned, possibly due to the deep desire to have their sister canonized. The Church demanded perfect virtue of the women saints, while accepting the human weakness, and even offensiveness in her men saints. St. Augustine in his *Confessions*, gives little evidence of being anything but a weak, albeit intellectually brilliant, man. Francis attests to his own sinfulness. However, with the exception of bodily ailments, church history has left us a Clare bereft of weakness and failure. Her endearing eccentricities inhabit the land of conjecture. We are left with a Clare of all light and no shadow. I cannot but wonder what happened to any written indication in Clare's own script which may have revealed her personal struggle with the demons of her own inner world. Perhaps this will never be known or proven. Nonetheless, Clare was not pure spirit. She shared human nature and thus shared in its brokenness and limitations, like the God she loved in Jesus. I doubt that Clare was perfectly virtuous. In one of his finer moments, Thomas Aquinas states that, "Grace builds upon nature." Clare is no exception to this maxim.

Clare lives on in human history for eight hundred years after her death. Many unanswered questions linger in the air, like incense clouding an altar. Did Clare miss her former way of life in the beginnings of her sisterly existence? Did she harbor desires of having her own little Franciscans running around her home? Did the apparent absence of her father leave her with a lack of an understanding of the masculine psyche? Did her heart yearn to be one with another? Were there times when she was tempted to kick the "obstinate" sisters not only out of community but solidly on their derrieres? Did she wrestle the inner demon of rage resultant upon the mutilation of her own and Francis's dream of a new model for living the Gospel? Was she angry with God for removing Francis from close proximity to her and her sisters? Were there times when she agonized over the clerical indications of women as being "lesser creations?" Did her deep grief, which her sisters reported upon her learning of the death of her beloved friend Francis, drive her to despair? Did the paralysis of fear grip her heart as she thought of traveling this world without the companionship of the one person who understood her soul and encouraged her heart, her soul mate Francis? Did confusion scramble her brain in its relentless drive to understand, organize, and explain that which could not yet be articulated in words? Did she ever want to give it up all up?

It is my conjecture that Clare learned by making a multitude of mistakes for which she needed to practice ongoing self-forgiveness. In one of the legends passed down, the devil appears to Clare and tells her that if she does not stop crying so profusely she will go blind. Tears of sadness? Frustration? Joy? Relief? Gratitude? Grief over the cruel treatment of both her Beloved Jesus and her beloved Francis? All possible and more, for tears are the language of the heart when words limit human expression of a deeply felt emotion. An example of Clare's learning from experience appears in her third letter to Agnes of Prague in which she encourages the princess to avoid extreme fasting. Karen Karper, in an article entitled 'Clare of Assisi: Spiritual Guide,' comments on Clare's own frailty due to her extreme fasting. Clare learned from the hard school of experience. Clare expresses that weakness is inherent in human nature, using this to discourage Agnes from harsh fasting. Karper says, "Clare understands full well, particularly through her own experience of twenty-eight years of chronic illness brought on, at least in part, through her own unwise zeal for fasting. In place of "an indiscreet and impossible austerity," she begs us in the Lord "to praise God by our very life, to offer to the Lord a reasonable service [Rm 12:1] and a sacrifice, "always seasoned with the salt of wisdom." [3L CL 40-41]

Clare managed to draw her community to a deeper awareness of their behaviors by emphasizing the silence of contemplative prayer, placing their "minds before the mirror of eternity," their souls before "the brilliance of glory," and their hearts "in the figure of the divine substance" (Cl 3). Karper further comments that, "Clare's use of the mirror symbol is taken from the spiritual literature of her day and is extremely rich and multifaceted. We look into a mirror not to see how we appear but to discover who we are and what we are to become."

The balance for this reflected image, should it be devastating to the beholder, comes from Clare's understanding of the human being who is "made to the image and likeness of God." She places her own humanness into the embrace of God and her community and invites the sisters to hold one another in the same embrace.

The Touch of Abbess

Clare joined Francis in 1212. In 1215, after much persuasive argument on the part of Francis, she accepted the title of Abbess, a title given to a superior in the Benedictine monasteries of women. Sister Pacifica de Guelfuccio, the first witness in the canonization process, attests to Clare's deep distaste for the position, commenting that, "...at the prayers and insistence of Saint Francis, who almost forced her, she accepted the direction and government of the sisters" (*ED*, 130). Was Clare so averse to becoming an abbess because it was considered a prestigious position?

Clare's passion, understood as an affection of the mind, and as suggested by J. Marvin Spiegelman in Jungian *Psychology and the Passions of the Soul* as an emotion which leads outward, incarnates in Clare's service to all who came for spiritual encouragement and material needs. Her sisters witness to the fact that Clare never asked a sister to do what she herself would not do, assisting with the manual labor in her early years of better health, then working on needlework projects when she became ill and bedridden. The role and accompanying prestige of Abbess placed her in a position over others. This no doubt was a hard pill for Clare to swallow. Nonetheless she did swallow it, making it a part of her own style of leadership in which she remained one among the many. One can only imagine Clare's confusion when Francis himself gave up his own leadership of the Brothers sometime before his own death in 1226. She, however, remained Abbess to her death in 1253. In her characteristic style of being sister and servant, Clare modeled rather than commanded. She advised and coaxed, rather than controlled and insisted. The *Process of Canonization* records the observations of Sister Amata regarding the character and effects of the leadership style of Clare. She witnesses that, "In her holiness, she governed herself and her sisters almost forty-three years. She loved the sisters as herself. The sisters held her in reverence as a saint and the mother of the entire Order both during her life and after her death." (*ED*, 157)

Yesterday touches Today

Leadership permeates Clare's experience of community. They are conjoined sides of the same reality. The community which surrounded Clare was invited to venture upon an odyssey that called forth a forgiving self-knowledge and a compassionate communal presence. Moreover, her style of leading encouraged the growth of a community of interdependence. The "shining star" syndrome found no home in her heart. All were responsible, all contributed talents and energy, all were sisters and, primarily, all were mystics in the sense of focused attention upon the centrality of love and Jesus Christ.

Clare was far ahead of her times. In the beginnings of my exploration, I stepped gingerly into her ideas of community. Then an unexpected fork appeared in the road, when my own community of Sisters asked that I take part in the weekend Leadership Seminar, discussed previously in this section. The seminar changed the direction of my study. I chose the road which clearly indicated that Clare's practice of communal leadership paralleled the newest findings in today's understanding of healthy organizational behaviors. In doing so, I am now led to a modern myth of David and Goliath in relation to the entrepreneurial movement taking its small smooth stones of individual ingenuity and creativity and taking slingshot aim at the corporate organizational giants of today. So did Clare in relation to the feudal system and Ecclesiastical Authority of her day. She modeled the technique which the seminar invited its participants to enter into; a weekend of a powerful and painful living of a technique which demanded constant presence to oneself within the context of a group.

A perspective from Ancient Greek Goddesses adds archetypal insights into her ideal of community. As the mythological Artemis chooses to dwell in the marshes between domesticated civilization and wild nature, so Clare chose the marshes outside of the city of Assisi. Clare's enclosed group consisted only of women; however, like Artemis, she befriended a great warrior: Artemis, Orion; Clare, Francis. Seduced by desire and the passion to propagate life in a spirit of joy, Aphrodite rises from the sea of Clare's longing for union and embodies an ideal alive and well in the lives of sisters and brothers who believe in Clare's joy in love and total dependence upon God. Hestia's fires of integrity and honesty, housed in the temples of the heart of Franciscans, burns steadily in their evangelical hearts the world over. Demeter looks for her lost daughter, abducted by the underworld, as Clare seeks out her daughters in the caverns of their own brokenness, abducted by the path of least resistance and the world's glamor. Clare's tears sound the cries of Persephone as she struggles with the ambiguities, confusions, and sadness of living in two worlds which are at odds with one another.

The Roman Catholic Church considers Clare to be the perfect imitator of Mary, the Mother of Jesus/God. However, the unique person of Clare can be defined by more than one religious tradition. She styles a form of life open to all who would venture the journey. Much like Jung's ideal notion of individuation, Clare's ideal of communal life is not meant for everyone to live out. However, it is a viable communal alternative among many possibilities, and fits well into the twenty-first century's endeavors to practice a new form of communal life. It models a style in which leadership dwells in the many, and mutual respect engenders freedom. Clare was after nothing less, and her first followers were after the same thing.

Release
Let go the clump,
burying the palm of peace-giving flesh.
Reach beyond the grasp that binds, offer the reach of kindly, tender touch.
Give to God the chunks of spoiled intent.
Pick up the shards of failed fantasies.
Bend your soul round the corners of new found, unbound twists and turns and trace a world open to the sweetness of a kiss.

BF

The Scent of Poverty: Simplicity
I came "into relationship" with poverty by coming through the back door of negative human emotions. It is these that I wrote about as my own experiences were perceived through the lens of poverty. What have emerged are feelings of confusion, disorientation, disorganization, dislocation and, finally, a sense of surrender. Fresh insights on the topic evaded me throughout the month of writing due to my dropping off and sorting out forty years of my own conscious and unconscious preconceptions of this all pervasive characteristic of Franciscan spirituality. I had originally hoped to avoid writing on the topic because it already fills volumes of manuscripts in libraries and archives throughout the western world. It seemed to me that enough had been said and is still being said about poverty. Like baggage on a train, it was to be packed

securely and respectfully far away from the dining car, where this study is fed; a silent and invisible companion on the way. A scholar in Franciscan Studies might smile indulgently over such naiveté and comment that, "Clare without poverty is like a fish without water, a book without words, a tree without branches." I might smile back and say, "But Clare is not about poverty. Clare is about love." However, here they are, more pages to add to the vast collection of black on white. Why?

Poverty has proven to be an enigma, occasioning deep disagreements and discussions among Franciscans from the time of Clare and Francis to this day. This is not the reason that moves me to write on poverty. My motivation arises from Clare's mothering of "the privilege of poverty" to her dying day. Her greatest joy was to kiss the document which held the written Church approval of her Rule. Locked within the textual prison of her Form of Life, which the Church refers to as a Rule, is the treasure of poverty whose only key is desire. The *Process of Canonization* records Clare's intense seduction by Lady Poverty in the testimony of Sister Filippa, who lived with Clare for thirty-eight years within the confines of San Damiano. It describes:

"At the end of her life, after calling together all her sisters, she entrusted the Privilege of Poverty to them. Her great desire was to have the Rule of the order confirmed with the papal Bull, to be able one day to place her lips upon the papal seal, and, then, on the following day, to die. It occurred just as she desired. She learned a brother had come with letters bearing the papal Bull. She reverently took it even though she was very close to death and pressed that seal to her mouth in order to kiss it. On the following day, Lady Clare died."

Judging from this testimony, Clare may not be about

poverty; however poverty is certainly about a Clare who embodied its evasive spirit, enfleshed its ghostlike appearance, and surrendered to its enticing simplicity. Its scent permeated the air she inhaled, entering her with its unpredictable and not always pleasant aromas. This is why I include it in this study.

Poverty, Natural and Deodorant -free

Viewing poverty as a gift and privilege was a new phenomenon in the late medieval period of Clare's life. The merchant class had burgeoned into a formidable opponent to the power and wealth of the nobility, and poverty was viewed as an evil to be avoided. The feudal system was dissolving like a mud wall in a rain storm, but the desire for power, wealth, and prestige flowed into the spirit of the new class. In the midst of this juggling of wealth, Clare and Francis advocated for poverty as a component of a new form of life in a community which chose to be dispossessed of all material things. Exalting poverty to the realm of nobility, Francis called her "Lady Poverty." She was to be respected as one worthy of honor and service. To this day, the Franciscan form of life is identified by the word poverty. What is the significance of the addition of the word "privilege" in Clare's version?

The word *privilege* denotes something that has a special immunity, or a right given to an individual. Immune from the dependency upon material possessions, Clare refused to wield power and control over anyone and anything. Therefore, the phrase *privilege of poverty* became her clarion call, and named her assurance that a kind and provident God would care for all her and her sisters' needs. It is this identification with poverty that most upset the clerics, nobles, and merchants of her day. In the midst of the chaos and uncertainty which plagued her times, Clare desired to exist simply as one of many who just wanted to live and let live. To strive not to better herself through climbing the ladder of fame and fortune appeared strange and mad to the people of her time. She in fact chose to step down from the economic and social ladder. On the one hand, Francis gave up something he was striving for: the dreams of knighthood and fame. On the other hand, Clare gave up the nobility and fame which were already hers by birthright. She chose to simply be a human being among the diverse creatures sharing the earth as their mother; natural and guileless, putting on no false airs, and smelling of themselves.

The Scent of Sea and Home

The following of Clare and Francis burgeoned in their own lifetimes. The Friars swelled to five thousand, and the Poor Ladies' monasteries numbered at least fifty-five. These numbers do not include the members of the affiliated groups scattered through Europe. Clare and Francis, like a medieval Odysseus and Penelope, set sail on the sea of poverty in different boats. Francis set his face outward to preaching in the townships of the Umbrian Mountains and beyond to the shores of the distant Holy Land and camps of the Saracens. On the other hand, Clare, like Penelope, remained in the enclosure of San Damiano for forty-two years, standing firm against the church authorities, which endeavored to fit this new spiritual phenomenon into the tradition of the centuries old Benedictine Rule. Furthermore, after Francis died in 1226, she supported her own and Francis's new communities as each struggled to find a way to live their calls into the future. Penelope had her suitors and pillagers. Clare had her ecclesiastics and noblemen. Clare, like Penelope, tended the home by journeying inward, weaving daily life into a tapestry of beginnings and endings, nightly destructions and morning's new beginnings integral to their work. Francis and Odysseus sailed into their journeys; ship-wrecked, beaten, and battered into their identities. However, Clare and Penelope knew who she was and remained steadfast in their determination to hold out to the end and/or their end. For forty-two years, Clare actively awaited the word that would give materiality to her Love, a living word that embodied the style of her loving. The assurance of poverty's progeny accompanied the approbation of her Form of Life. Furthermore a personal identity became a communal identity which penned a new myth, that of the Myth of Lady Poverty. "Poor" named the ground of the story in which Clare's vision was planted. Clare was the scent of home that drew poverty to take root. Clare and poverty tended the human plants which grew in the enclosed garden of San Damiano, where poverty had become a living symbol in the person of Lady Clare Offreduccio

A living symbol, like a living person, takes on the ability to evolve beyond its first manifestation. How might this evolution occur in reference to an image? In the compendium of his essays entitled, *Gaston Bachelard, On Poetic Imagination and Reverie*, Bachelard contends that any psychology which focuses only on the constitution of images, and does not consider the "*mobility of images*" is missing half of the formula needed, "for essential *newness* that characterizes the human psyche" (10). The chapter entitled "Creative Imagination and Language," contains excerpts from an essay titled *L'invitation au voyage* [Italicized in the text]. Within the broader context of his theory that an image is not a picture, but an experience; it lives. He explains:

"For a complete psychology, imagination is, above all, a type of spiritual mobility, the model of the greatest, the liveliest, the most living mobility. We must therefore systematically add to the study of a particular image the study of its mobility, its fertility, its life..."

Carrying through on the thought of Bachelard, that image is mobile, I contend that Clare's notion of poverty which she shared with Francis, symbolized a living and growing image which existed beyond the imagination of one human being. Poverty became a "she." Furthermore, she took on the nobility of a feudal lady dressed in rags uncharacteristic of the social standing of a noble lady. Poverty's mobility not only changed her in status and gender, but also in reproductive potential. She has become the "Lady" of all the Friars, and the subsequent children who follow the lifestyle of Clare and Francis. She is mobile, fertile, and living.

The active interchange between the living Clare and living poverty transformed both in the exchange. Clare loaned poverty the trapping of her "Ladyship" and poverty showed Clare how to surrender to divine providence. Furthermore, Clare saw through poverty's self-chosen place as an outsider, and brought her solitude and silence into the convent of San Damiano where she became an insider. Within an ecclesial and social milieu which despised poverty, Clare reintroduced the truth and beauty of the simplicity of dispossession, and refused to be misled by any talk of discretion and forethought, practicing what she advised Agnes to do in her Second Letter. Clare encourages Agnes to follow in the footprints of the one she loves, and further urges:

Unswervingly seek poverty - Remember Him.
Be aware of Him.
Journey on swiftly, keeping hold of your aim,
With lightness of step and freedom of movement
swiftly keep moving.
Let no dust collect in your steps on the path of
happiness.
Go carefully, securely, joyfully.
Let nothing block the way on which the Spirit of the
Lord has called you to embrace the Poor Christ.
As a poor and obedient virgin embrace the poor
Christ.
Gaze long at Him-the poor contemned Christ . . .
Ponder and weigh in your heart and contemplate Him,
your Beloved.

(trans. Clare Agnes, O.S.C. CL 4)

Clare encourages Agnes to walk a course of happiness, repeating her exhortation to draw and remain close to the poor Christ. Being poor and being happy constitute the two sides of Clare's coin of love. These are oppositional only in so far as they show two facets of the same reality, like the opposite sides of a coin. Clare, eighteen years older than Agnes, mentors her new sister into the light side of poverty. Negative destitution is a prevailing image of poverty, the sense that it is only lack. Clare shows Agnes that this is a faulty view. Clare transforms the image of a poverty which she portrays as a helpful companion. She reshapes it by correcting what she considers a misshapen perception. To Clare, poverty offered superfluity, not lack; freedom, not bondage. To Clare, Francis, and their original followers only total dispossession showed poverty in her full beauty, and opened one to see that there is enough for all. However, Lady Poverty kept moving and changing.

Women and men not called to be a friars or nuns requested direction on how they might seek God in the manner of Clare and Francis. Between 1209 and 1216, the notion of poverty expanded to include them. They had children to tend to, businesses to guide, farms to manage, homes to take care of. It is through them that simplicity of lifestyle while living in the marketplace entered the domain of poverty. This choice demands conscious awareness of those who are poorer and those who suffer most deprivation in any area of human experience: material, spiritual, psychological, and physical. Does this glorify suffering for suffering's sake?

Commitment to the divestment of poverty may appear to be the choice of pain. To some, suffering is unendurable, to others it is just another unexpected bend in the road of life. Whatever the viewpoint, this world and her people suffer, and life on earth is not perfect. To most human beings this is a given. Clare, whose name means "light, clear," chose to map her life through the worst of human experiences, and awaken herself into its deepest potential - union with God. This journey leads her through the darkness and stenches of persecution, loneliness, grief, fear, and despair. Whatever Clare experienced turned into light not by destroying its nature, but by incorporating it and introducing all to the greater light, like the glow of a candle in the noonday sun. Poverty is the candlelight; Jesus Christ, the Sun.

Poverty has remained an enigma throughout the eight hundred years of Franciscan history, in spite of all efforts to see beyond her dark trappings and into the lightness of her burden. Early followers of Francis decried poverty's profanation. Twentieth-century interpretations see poverty as a simplicity of life style and solidarity with the poor in their struggle for justice and peace. I liken poverty to the limburger cheese of the Franciscan diet. Poverty is a food for the spirit upon which the nose and taste do not agree. My Austrian and Swiss mother appreciated its cheesy secret, not bothered by its scent. However, when a member of my family opened the refrigerator, it spoke a loud and clear message of "stink." If mom had shopped that day, the smell of limburger cheese escaped with a force strong enough to throw the door opener against the opposite wall. At least, that is how everyone else in the family felt. Later in my life, while holding my nose closed, I tasted a small morsel of this olfactory villain. It was delicious. I now eat limburger cheese. So why such an image?

Clare expected that in the daily rounds of life, some situations would smell of roses and others of garbage. One is fragrant and the other stinks, and God is in them both. Lepers did not smell good. Herein lies the secret that is not a secret, which is named poverty. Life offers a diversity of scents and we humans respond in a multitude of ways. However, the inspiration passed on by Clare and Francis is that God is in it all. In their chosen belief system, God entered the whole of the human experience in the person of Jesus Christ, therefore proclaiming all of creation to be holy. To argue this point is not the goal of this writer. It is simply to state what is basic to the nature of Clare's way of life. Furthermore, although Clare is the center of this work, she cannot be separated from Francis in their shared focus on God incarnated, and following Jesus' way of living to the letter as described in the Gospels. These are shared realities to each of them. Then why does the subject of poverty remain consistently in the forefront of Franciscan dialogue? Jesus saying "Sell your possessions, and give to the poor... then come back and follow me" (Mathew 19: 21) seems a straight forward message. Does poverty demand the literal interpretation of Christ's words as understood by the original sisters and brothers? Does it mean "simplicity of life style" as understood by writers like Audrey Gibson and Kieran Kneaves, who, in their book *Praying with Louise de Marillac* say of it:

"Simplicity means that we live close enough to the limits of our resources so that we can rely on God's providence and appreciate the beauty of life. Simplicity fosters spontaneity, truthfulness, and clear speech. Simplicity also is required of anyone who seeks justice, peace, and equitable stewardship of resources. Simplicity is not a simple way to live. It requires serious reflection to sort out what is necessary and what is luxury."

There is no evidence in Clare's writings that she believed that poverty should be understood only as she practiced it. She encouraged freedom of choice. However, if women chose to follow her ideal, it was expected that they have a keen sense and clear understanding of what they were committing themselves to. Only after a time of formation were they admitted into the enclosed community. In other words, her style was not for everyone. This said, rather than an either/or attitude toward these two views of simplicity or total divestment, I see poverty from a both/and/plus stance. I see that poverty includes the possibilities of divesting oneself of all material possessions for the love of God, choosing the ongoing simplicity of life in the marketplace, plus the desire to surrender to life. Poverty, whether it be spiritual or material, belongs to everyone. It is Clare and Francis who gave poverty back to humanity. The shape of its practice remains a personal, and in the case of religious congregations, a communal choice. Their new vision includes tenets like: poverty exalts, not degrades; is simple, not cluttered; is generous, not grasping; is creative, not lazy; is joyful, not de-energizing. Most prominent in its effects is the growth of the person into her/his best human potential. In this list I am speaking of an ideal. An ideal, in the experience of living, is sought and attained fully or partially. Nonetheless, the fact that one woman and man lived that ideal to its utmost, cannot be denied. If a dream is lived, it exists on the material plane. Poverty is possible for all. It motivates one to a sense of gratitude and dependence upon a loving Creator-God, and loving that Creator and all created in return. The practice of poverty is to remind us of the abundance of life as gift given. If these result from a focused simplicity of life, then Clare's ideal of poverty is served.

The Smell of Fear

Horror movies portray human beings stricken into immobility, eyes wide with terror. Piercing screams tell the viewer that something frightful is happening. The audience partakes of this banquet of fear. It is likely that, if asked, most of the spectators would agree that courage in the face of torment, torture, and adversity is remarkable in any place and in any era, as it was in third-century Carthage, when a group of Christians were led out into an arena to face wild beasts and ultimate death. Marie Anne Mayeski, in *Women Models of Liberation*, narrates the story of a noble woman among these early Christians, twenty years of age and a recent mother of a baby boy, who was arrested along with her child. Anxious over the wellbeing of her child, she eventually gave him over to the care of his grandmother, to be taken to the prison only when needing to be nursed.

This prisoner's name was Vibia Perpetua and her crime was professing to be a Christian during a time and in a place deeply hostile toward the sect. Her aged father repeatedly visited her in prison, begging that she not dishonor the family and abandon her baby. Her father's pleas did not stop Perpetua from refusing publicly to reject Christianity, as was demanded by the governor Hilarion. During her imprisonment, Perpetua wrote an account of her experiences up to the time of entering the arena. Describing her first impressions of the dungeon prison she writes:

"I was terrified because never before had I experienced such darkness. What a terrible day! Because of crowded conditions and rough treatment by the soldiers the heat was unbearable. My condition was aggravated by my anxiety for my baby."

The ensuing paragraphs speak of her love for her child and concern over the physical and social stresses placed upon her aging father due to her choice to remain Christian. Words flow out in streams of vivid description as she writes about the routines and conditions within the jail, the behaviors of the guards, and the courage of other prisoners, many of whom were her friends. Later in her journal, Perpetua reports that, "Suddenly the prison became my palace, and I loved being there rather than any other place." This extreme reversal of attitude resulted in part from a sense of community and shared plight, which emerged within the confines of the prison enclosure, transforming it from dungeon to palace. Companionship re-enforced the change. Perpetua, like Clare, was divested of all past experiences and relationships. Although one chose divestment freely and the other by force, they shared a mutual result of joy within their total vulnerability. Both perceived gain in their loss. What did Perpetua hope to gain?

Perpetua's record of her own visions and dreams and those of other prison inmates gives glimpses into the inner lives of her co-inmates and the source of their courage. These shared dreams encouraged fortitude and perseverance. Saturus, whom Perpetua refers to as "brother," shared with her the story of one of his visions. It prefigures a future, at the end of their sufferings. In it, he and Perpetua are caught into an upward movement beyond the earth's atmosphere into a brilliant light where Saturus says to Perpetua, "This is what the Lord promised. We have received his promise." The vision goes on to describe a lush landscape with tall trees, blossoming roses, and flowers of every variety. Here they are greeted by friends who preceded them in death. Four angels then herald their arrival with jubilation saying, "Here they are. They have arrived." Amid the sounds of a continuous chant of praise, they are presented before the throne of a white haired man whose face appears young, and who is flanked on either side by a host of elders. The man with the white hair gently strokes their faces, a tender gesture which they in turn pass on to others in the form of the kiss of peace. Saturus then says to Perpetua, "You have your wish." She answered, "I thank God, for although I was happy on earth, I am much happier here right now."

Following these words, they go out and meet the bishop Optatus and the priest Aspasius. These men kneel before the two saying, "Make peace between us for you've gone away and left us this way." Humbled by the bishop's and priest's kneeling before them, they all begin to talk together. Angels interrupt their conversation with words of advice to forgive one another and heal dissentions among them. Perpetua and Saturus then recognize other of their friends and the vision ends in a joyous reunion. Saturus's experience of those last moments is recorded by Perpetua. She writes, "We were all sustained by an indescribable fragrance which completely satisfied us. Then in my joy, I awoke."

In the dank environs of prison, Saturus's sustenance for life took on the sense of a scent. It permeated the surrounding air and entered deeply into that which is life replenishing. Perhaps he experienced what is known as "the odor of sanctity," which is recorded as hovering in the air upon the death of a saint. But does scent carry more than an odor? Does it also create a spirit that lingers after the scent is gone? Some scholars seem to think so.

David Miller, in confronting the modern day's strictly rational and compartmentalized approaches to theologizing, attempts in his book, *Christs*, to transfuse heavy doses of literary and mythological corpuscles into the cold body of theological academia. The disciplines of psychology, literature, and mythology are used to show that theological education and religious tradition have something to gain from an interdisciplinary approach toward learning. In Part 2: "Christ, The Clown", Miller suggests that the contemporary scene has lost its nose, or its ability to come to an insight by sniffing it out. The nose is of special interest to Miller, who focuses on smells as being an indication that spirit does have an odor, in spite of its corporality. Chapter 14, "The Smell of Traditional Religion and its Mythic Under-Odor," names works written between the tenth and nineteenth centuries which speak of odors coming from the dead bodies of saints, referring specifically to *Selectum martyra acta;* Baeda's *Ecclesiastical History;* Mallory's *Morte d'Arthur;*

Fioretti's *Opera*; and Voltaire's poem about Joan of Arc *La Pucelle*. Miller further cites examples from the works of Dostoyevsky, Sir Walter Scott, Swedenborg, and R. A. Vaughan, noting that the scent of death threads through the literature of the ages. The point of his observations is to emphasize that there is written evidence which recognizes that spirit does have a scent. Miller's interest is with the topic's reoccurrence, not with the factual proof of the phenomenon. On page 85 of the book, he suggests that, "... religious significance is sensed by smell," and that, "It is basic to religious tradition." He further notes that, "In addition to incense there is another 'smell' in the history of religion," referring to the odor of sanctity, which describes the scent emitted from holy persons' bodies at the time of their death. However, scent can be as tricky as the god Hermes. Corrupting flesh naturally smells worse than acrid, yet there is about some bodies a pleasant scent; dungeons and prisons smell rank, yet Saturus inhales a memorably heavenly scent; limburger cheese offends the nose, yet rests deliciously upon the palette. These are reversals of the expected, and in that, possess the mysterious aroma of Lady Poverty.

Poverty is as close to life as a breath. She translates into a diversity of odors. In a sniff, she enters and rides on the current of the surrounding air, an uninvited guest who brings baggage reeking with the stench of gaseous chemicals or exuding the fragrance of wild roses and lavender. In the Franciscan tradition, she cannot be avoided, because her founder Francis traces his conversion to the time when he was able to kiss the rotting lips of a leper. His transformation began with the stench of corruption, not the sweet fragrance of perfume. On the other hand, Clare describes scent as an active and regenerating power from a smell pleasing to the senses. In her fourth letter to Agnes, she includes an extravagant description of their Beloved:

"Happy, indeed, is she to whom it is given to share this sacred banquet, to cling with all her heart to Him... Whose beauty all the heavenly hosts admire unceasingly... Whose graciousness is our joy. . . Whose gentleness fills us to overflowing. . . Whose remembrance brings a gentle ligh...*Whose fragrance will revive the dead"*... [Writer's Italics]." (CL 4, *F/C* 204)

"To revive the dead" is a powerful image. The dead to whom Clare refers may be those whose spirit no longer energizes their person, as in the deeply depressed. It may also mean the termination of life as understood by mortals. She gives no indication of what she may mean other than using the word *revive* rather than *raise*. In Clare's chosen mythology, that is the Gospels, Jesus is recorded to have raised an only son of a widowed mother, a young girl child, and his friend Lazarus, and then is raised himself after dying on a cross. Added to this was her belief that Jesus Christ resurrected himself by reclaiming his God nature, thereby redefining who God is and might be. Perhaps Clare saw that reviving the dead is no less powerful than raising the dead, which she leaves to her God. Whatever her intent, death is a shared human experience. It divests the person of material trappings, robbing her of participation in the exchange of life between itself and the universe, a heart throbbing with life in an unconscious exchange of oxygen and carbon dioxide. There is no greater poverty than death. It is the ultimate destitution. Although Clare prayed healing for some who asked her, and they were healed, there is no evidence that she raised anyone from the dead. This is significant to what Clare may have meant by the phrase

"To revive the dead." It could allude to the revival of spirit in those who have lost who they are and suffered the consequences of dying to all of importance in their lives, especially the feelings of belonging and love.

Everyday life might give some examples of Clare's notion of revivals. A sister with whom I live uses garlic to flavor almost every dish she cooks. When I walk through the front door after an exhausting day at work, the pungent aroma saturating the air revives memories of my childhood. My mom cooks again, and through a process like osmosis, my Lebanese ancestry seeps through my tissues and my mouth waters with anticipation of the meal awaiting me. On the other hand, Jelaluddin Rumi sees garlic when it has lost it scent, much like Miller's comments about losing sniffing power. The garlic can no longer smell its own being into mouth-watering desire. Rumi writes about the cause and effect of this loss:

An Empty Garlic, You miss the garden,
because you want a small fig from a random tree.
You don't meet the beautiful woman. You're joking
with an old crone. It makes me want to cry how she
detains you, stinking mouthed, with a hundred talons,
putting her head over the roof edge to call down,
tasteless fig, fold over fold, empty as dry-rotten garlic.
She has you tight by the belt, even though there's no
flower and no milk inside her body. Death will open
your eyes to what her face is: leather spine of a black
lizard. No more advice. Let yourself be silently drawn
by the stronger pull of what you really love.

(Barks 37)

Rumi begins by describing an overlooked garden,

therefore enjoyed neither in sight nor in scent. Love's silent beckoning and its seductive attraction await conscious recognition. Clare, on the other hand, aware of both the garden and the love, did not allow the stinking mouthed, ecclesiastical crones to distract her in her pursuit. The church leadership did not understand Clare, or in understanding too much saw the dangerous need to change their personal lives and the monarchy of the church. It may have been both. Whatever that may have been, Clare's centered love for God strengthened her. Poverty was a means to open her to that love, but it was never an end in itself. It mattered little that sometimes love appeared in dry, rotten, and tasteless outer trappings. Love led her to choose its difficult yet simple way because, like the work of the alchemist as described by Edward Edinger in *Anatomy of the Psyche*, she was: "...committed to a sacred work - a search for the supreme and ultimate value" (5). Furthermore, Sister Karen Karper claims that Clare's poverty is, "...a royal way to and from the heart of God." Humility and faith are its companions on the road, and contemplation is its offspring. These are easy words when articulated from the refined and privileged place of nobility. However, what did this mean to the Clare who tended the rotting and stench ridden flesh of lepers, inhaled the dank air of the marshy surroundings of San Damiano, whiffed the odors of unbathed bodies in close proximity to one another, and met the relentless demands of the daily household tasks? What alchemy of spirit accompanied her through her struggles to walk peacefully with Lady Poverty?

The Scent of History
It is paramount at this point to contextualize poverty

historically before proceeding to look at the alchemy of Clare's spirit. Today, the worldwide Franciscan family is comprised of three groups within the organizational structure of today's Catholic Church: the First Order of ordained priests; the Second Order, cloistered nuns, and The Third Order. The last is subdivided into The Third Order Regulars who profess permanent vows in religious communities and work among the people, and the Secular Franciscan Order (SFO) who choose to live the Franciscan ideal within their professions and commitments in the outside world either in the married, clerical, or single state. At the beginning of the new millennium, Lester Bach, O.F.M. Cap. (Order of Friars Minor, Capuchins), rewrote the study guide entitled *Catch Me a Rainbow Too - The Franciscan Journey*, which is used in the formation of those interested in becoming members of the SFO. This group includes those who are unable to become friars or Poor Clares but who want to live the spirits of poverty and simplicity in their lives. Lester summarizes the history of these Secular Franciscans, placing them in the framework of the medieval era. He states that penitents wandered throughout Europe in the twelfth and thirteenth centuries, and explains further:

"They performed works of charity, wore special clothing and were dedicated to personal conversion. Some among them were extreme and heretical. Others were moderate and orthodox. When Francis sent his first group of followers on a preaching trip, he called them "The Penitents from Assisi."

Mention of these groups within the Franciscan tradition is necessary for an expanded view of professed poverty. Followers of the Franciscan ideal numbered persons from the lowest step of economic wealth to the highest; from the impoverished to the wealthiest, from the landed lord to the farming peasant: among the latter the simple farm couple, Luchsio and Bonadonna of Poggibonsi, whom Francis himself invested; Princess Elizabeth of Hungary, mother of four; Angela of Foligno, known as "Teacher of Theologians"; Margaret of Cortona, neglected as a child and converted from a life of prostitution; Louis IX, King of France, father of eleven children; and more modern day Matt Talbot, who suffered from alcoholism. It is no wonder that poverty appears as an enigma to the very people who claim her as their standard bearer. What is the common denominator which poverty embodies for these and the present day's diversity of members in the Franciscan Family?

Thaddeus Horgan, a Franciscan scholar and priest, offers some light on the contradiction between poverty's interpretations as total material divestment or natural simplicity of lifestyle. In a compendium of his articles gathered into a booklet entitled *Turned to the Lord*, Horgan dedicates this writing to coworkers, called the groupe de travail, of the International Franciscan Commission who, together with him from 1979-1981, developed reflections on the main themes of Franciscan spirituality. It became one of the four documents used as a reference for writing a renewed Rule for the Third Order Regular of St. Francis. In an article entitled "Gospel Poverty: Life's Sufficiency," Horgan suggests that poverty grows from an attitude of inadequacy concerning the things of God, and an in-depth conviction of "needing God." This is reminiscent of the first tenet of Alcoholics Anonymous, which admits to a powerlessness over alcohol and a need for a higher power to help combat it. Examples of this vulnerable state are evident in everyday experiences, like that of Martin, whose cancer is now making its final claim on his life.

For the first time in the year and a half of our walking the cancer journey together, Martin admitted in a recent phone conversation, "Barbara, I give up. I just give up." He asked that I come to see him, but explained, "I am too weak to talk today." Martin's greatest joy is found in a good discussion and shared ideas. However, he is now adrift on an ocean of cancer and has no physical or psychological resources remaining in the weakened boat of his body. With his body in retrograde, his spirit balances somewhere between now and forever. Poverty faithfully accompanies Martin through the alchemy of the dying process. This is one face of Lady Poverty often neglected and denied, and understandably so. Who of humankind wants to admit the abrupt entrance of "Sister Death," as she is called by Francis. She is known of, but not about, in the sense of personal experience. This occurs only in each person's dying. Her total emptying of the human physical container constitutes the limits of all divestment. Yet, on her own deathbed, Clare spoke consoling words of encouragement to her own soul as this specter approached:

"Go in peace, because you will have a good escort. The One Who created you has already provided that you will be made holy. The One Who created you has infused the Holy Spirit in you and then guarded you as a mother does her littlest child." (Sister Benvenuta, *ED* 162)

For Clare, as for Francis, a greater energy carried them beyond their bodies and materiality. To them, God was their chosen Higher Power and was greater than sickness, starvation, persecution, and death. Furthermore, the figure of Jesus Christ as God-made-man, drew them to an incarnate God, that is to say, an entirely enfleshed and human God. Jesus Christ absorbed their minds and fueled their imaginations. According to Horgan, herein lies the genius of Francis: he studied Jesus' life from the Gospels, and found a God who claimed a human body as home. He grasped that part of Jesus' life called incarnation and took it seriously. Jesus was birthed, gave his parents problems, developed into a mature man, attended weddings, ate good food, drank wine, formed relationships, felt rejected, became angry, was betrayed by a friend, was imprisoned and tortured, then died on a cross. In the Catholic Tradition, the threefold combination of Jesus' life, death, and resurrection form a unified whole, but the part of that totality which intrigued Francis was the material life of the God-made-man. A disembodied spirituality finds no place in the Clare's or Francis's ways. Body and spirit, materiality and spirituality, creation and humanity, flesh and soul, emotion and intellect, unite as one. They manifest a Creator who is beyond imagination. Therefore the gospel myth of Jesus Christ is central to them because it is the only source of seeing what a human relationship with God might look like. However, if all is one and holy, then why choose to live in poverty? It appears that the very creation seen to be a manifestation of God obstructs the way to that God. Strange paradox. Clare is a woman of paradoxes.

Clare is remembered by her sisters and friends as being a happy and joyful person. Abnegation is not emphasized in Clare's own extant writings. The letters to Agnes of Prague, the Form of Life, the Testimony, and final Blessing for her sisters portray a woman of positive attitudes, honest speech, imaginative words, and encouraging advice. Above all, she is grateful. Her deathbed prayer is, "Thank you for my life." In exalting poverty, she consistently points toward a path of joy and "prudent happiness," particularly in her third letter to Agnes of Prague where she exclaims:

> …May you be very joyful in the Lord!
> Be not entangled with bitterness or a cloud of sadness.
> Joy! that you are in Christ, redeemed.
> Joy! in your well-being.
> Joy! in your happiness.
> Joy! in your progress, your growth.
> …Joy! That you work with God Himself to support the weak and falling.
> Joy!... (Clare Agnes O.S.C 7)

Clare is not the only one who found that joy accompanies poverty. Leslie A. Fiedler, in the introduction to a book of collected letters and essays written by Simone Weil entitled, *Waiting For God*, lists three factors present in Weil's interest in myth, one of which parallels Clare's judgment that poverty and joy are related. One factor arises from Weil's mentor, Plato, who "at all great crises of his thought falls back on the mythic in search of a subtle and total explication…" Secondly, Fiedler sees Weil as thinking that the archetypal poetics of different cultures come from the same truths, expressed in "different metaphoric languages." Thirdly, Weil is thought to believe that only the poor will recognize myth's potential. It is here where Clare and Weil agree. Fiedler states:

"…there is her sense of myth as the special gospel of the poor, a treasury of insights into the Beauty of the World, which Providence has bestowed on poverty alone, but which, in our uprooted world, the alienated oppressed can no longer decipher for themselves."

It seems paradoxical that a Jewish woman of the

twentieth century who chose not to be baptized into the Catholic Church, and who believed that her vocation was to be an "outsider," should have a grasp on the spirit of Clare's perception of poverty, which is central to the Gospel identified as Good News. The good news is vested in the "Beauty of the world," and the joy resultant upon the choice of voluntary poverty. Furthermore, the chosen leader of the Christian community, Jesus, is pictured as a man who preached good news and encouragement to the poor. Weil catches his message and carries the ball further by discussing how thought blossoms not from gritting the teeth and enduring the suffering of a forced power of will, but comes to fullness in the presence of joy. She says that, "The intelligence can only be led by desire. For there to be desire, there must be pleasure and joy in the work. The intelligence only grows and bears fruit in joy."

Clare contemplatively placed her mind before the mirror of eternity, as she told Agnes to do. Her joy was to walk the highway of poverty to reach the source of her desire, God. She had much to give away and give up as a noblewoman in the Middle Ages. Descriptions of the struggles to do so are present in their absence from her writings. She turned wealth into poverty and never missed what is perceived as "the good life" of material superfluity or even sufficiency. This is because Clare looked upon life with eyes that registered only abundance. Life is abundance. How can she or anyone miss something that they do not perceive themselves as lacking? This is Clare's secret of poverty, which is not a secret. But it did not happen overnight.

Poverty's Lonely Waiting Game
Waiting is a kind of poverty whose way is recognized

by writers who struggle to transfer thought to paper. It is like a dry thirsting woman traveling through a desert, trudging her route between watering places, and accompanied only by silence. The thirst occurs, the silence prevails, and the journey encompasses now and forever. There is a sense of "Will this never end?" Perhaps this attitude signals a disconnection with the passion that gives energy for the writing. Toil has replaced it. No organized pattern of thought hammers together a basic framework upon and around which ideas congregate. It is un-excavated earth, awaiting a blueprint. At these times, willpower may see it through to the end, but hazards the risk of becoming lifeless and scentless. Simone Weil in *Waiting for God* captures the ideal of waiting while the thought makes its way to articulation. She believes:

"There is a way of giving our attention to the data of a problem in geometry without trying to find the solution or to the words of a Latin or Greek text without trying to arrive at the meaning, a way of waiting, when we are writing, for the right word to come of itself at the end of our pen, while we merely reject all other words."

Accompanying waiting is the long loneliness of being prepared at any time for the lover to return, the child to get home at night, the call from a friend, the results of medical tests, the birth of a grandchild, the job interview, the return of a term paper, or the inevitable call of death. History does not record Clare's long wait for the church and even her own followers' understanding of her own and Francis's ideal of poverty. She waited twenty-seven years for the "right word to come of itself at the end of the pen," first in her own Rule written one year before her death, then in the word of Church's approval of that Rule in 1253, the year of her death. What about the long loneliness between the death of her friend Francis in 1226 and her own death in 1253? What was it like?

Robinson Jeffers in his poem story, 'The Loving Shepherdess,' captures the essence of Clare's lonely journey. In a fresh approach toward the felt reality of loneliness which only poetry frees into understanding, Jeffers narrates the story of a woman, named Clare Walker, who appropriately lives into the fullness of her name. She shepherds a flock of sheep which she walks through the journey of the poem. Her migrations are set mainly in northern California. Unlike Clare Offreduccio, Clare Walker moves freely, never staying in one place, meeting an assortment of kind, bitter, generous, spiteful, and abusive people. She narrates the past episodes in her life with dispassionate detachment: a lover abandons her after killing her father and leaves her to take the blame for the death, her miscarriage of her child, and neighbors who leave her to isolating loneliness. She is considered insane. Clare lets go of all she knows and she begins her journey with a small flock of sheep, absorbed in the task of caring for them. Clare portrays total vulnerability and an open and unjudgemental love which is so accepting that this reader wondered if the shepherdess was, in fact, insane. However, in the midst of her wanderings and meetings along the way, Clare expresses truths with the clarity of a seer tied to the fact of human flesh. When talking with Vasquez, a dreamy cattleman who cares for Clare during one of her illnesses, she insists that her dreams are not of the quality of useless visions but on the other hand exclaims, "Oh no, it was nothing," she said, "in the way of that. Visions? My trouble is a natural thing" (218). Later in their conversation, youthful Vasquez listens as Clare questions:

"Have you never seen in your visions

The golden country where our souls came from,
Before we looked at the moon and stars and knew they
are not perfect?
We came from a purer peace..."

Vasquez affirms that he has dreams of a place before
the present and he replies that, "...We shall return there, we
homesick." However Clare counters with, "No" ...the place
was my mother's body before I was born. You may
remember it a little but I've remembered plainly," and goes
on to explain, "...but after a while you'll remember plainly,
if some long trouble makes you want peace; or being
handled has broken your shame. I have no shame now."
Clare Walker's experiences are of the earth's making:
experiences of shameful events which destroy all shame,
and the womb of mother earth's body. No visions in the
vaporous visitations which Vasquez doubts, although a
recipient of such dreams, have any use in this life. On the
other hand, Clare's wisdom taps into the truths that lie
buried in earth and childbirth, recollecting memories of her
first stillborn child. Her roots cling deeply to earth; her
mind unwilling to move into the world of spirit without
grounding. Earth is her heaven because it is her fleshly
home. She longs for the birthing of life in carnate form and
sees in it the wonder of ongoing fruition. In truth, Clare
carries another child within her and knows that the birthing
will kill her. In the end, at feeling a second labor pain, "She
crept down to the river and hid her body in the willow
thick. In the evening, between the rapid summits of agony
before exhaustion, she called the sheep about her and
perceived that none came."
Not having shifted to my mind and sifted the poem
through my brain, I simply and quietly wept when I first

read it. This Clare Walker reminded me of Clare of Assisi, who symbolized a haven for the frightened men and women who were caught like sheep among a warring Emperor and Pope, nobility, and merchant class. The folks wanted to till and eat the fruits of that land over which their battles were fought. Present-day African and South American nations suffer the same oppression as the lands are ravaged by war and terrorism, world powers destroying the earth under their feet for the sake of economic and political sovereignty. This is no different from Clare's own day of warring communes and bloody crusades. Not a great deal has changed for the poor and voiceless in any country in today's market economy.

Onorio Vasquez coaxed Clare Walker to come home with him to his family, whose father would be her father and whose brothers would be her brothers. He describes a place where her sheep would have pasture, and the beauty of the land would heal her spirit. Clare Walker would have none of it. She thanked him and later said, "If I go up to Calvary ten million times: what is that to you? Let me go up." Clare's courage moved Vasquez. He sought to find a place where they could simply live and be. What Vasquez desired was to live in tranquility, enjoying the simple comforts of an existence surrounded by loved ones and working the good land. But there are some persons called out from security and contentment to live deeper or higher; to live a life beyond themselves and beyond others. I grieved Clare Walker's losses. I grieved over her hardships and the cruelties she encountered along the way. I wept that she did not finally say yes to Vasquez, and settle into a temporary place of sojourn in order to find some happiness here on earth. I disliked her choice of wanting to be born again, out from the mother womb where she lay down to die like a grain of wheat. I grieved what could have been. I am touched by such total focus and abandonment to destiny. I now recognize and grieve the losses that Clare of Assisi's choice of life may have cost her as a human being.

Clare of Assisi's choices marked her as a woman of intense purpose. Her persistent choice of material divestment, like that of Jeffers' Clare, led her on a road less traveled, a road which demanded ongoing movement toward one goal. For Clare, that goal was total identification with her Beloved. Poverty was the means. Were there another means, Clare would have taken it for love alone. The union of love to Love was her aim. Clare of Assisi resembled Clare Walker in the focused and dedicated resolve to become one within the place from whence she took her life, the mother-womb or in other words the earth flesh from which she came. Clare of Assisi differed from Walker in that the burning focus of her focus was totally toward union with the God from whence she came. She discovered God in the heart of material creation. Both women chose the way of self-surrender and care for what is beyond their own comfort. Both women's troubles began the day they fled from the security of their homes and chose to live as outcasts beyond the protection of established society. Both portrayed shades of the goddess Artemis, because they chose to live away from the cities, in the wilds between civilization and nature. These are places of solitude. It is this aspect of Clare's need which drove her to dwell with wild creatures in the marshlands outside the city walls of Assisi. The two Clares counted their sacrifices as nothing in the light of their burning desires. What for most would be loneliness, for them was fullness. Poverty again turns the ordinary view of an unacceptable experience into one of simple necessity. Loneliness accompanies desire, and passion outshines the light of simple companionship; strange bedfellows.

Breathing Free

There is another aspect of poverty which turns the ordinary notion of what it is into the opposite of that notion; its sometimes acrid scent into an experience of sweetness. One such reversal is the connection of poverty with freedom. Its liberating angle is not unique to Clare and Francis in the twelfth century. Marie Louise von Franz, in *Psyche and Matter,* discusses the works of a medieval monk and respected scholar, the Abbot Joachim da Fiori, who died in 1202. Among his theories is one in which he divides history into three eons; the first being that of the Father of the Old Testament; the second that of the Son, being the First Christian Millennium; and the third of the Holy Ghost, being the time "in which spiritual man will live in poverty but in complete freedom following the inspiration of the Holy Ghost." Jung also discusses the ideas of Joachim of Flora within the context of a commentary on the influence of astrological foretellings on historical events. In his work *Aion,* Jung reports that the ideas of Joachim were condemned by the Fourth Lateran Council 1215. He goes on to say that as late as 1254, a Franciscan friar, Gerard of Borgo San Donnino, claimed that Jaochim's historical paradigm was equivalent to a new Gospel. Another contemporary of Clare and Francis was the philosopher and monk, Almaric of Bene, who died in 1204, and was condemned for his teachings concerning the new age and movement of the Holy Ghost connecting freedom and poverty. New attitudes towards the practice of poverty permeated the era of Francis and Clare. What emergent understandings led to the upsurge of interest in the practice of poverty? I believe that the twelfth and thirteenth centuries fomented in a cauldron of a new-found freedom which allowed ideals such as poverty to break through old patterns of thoughts into new expressions of insight. The human mind was changing along with the economic and political systems. Poverty was viewed as a way of sharing the goods of the earth among the varied communities of humankind. It was envisioned as a choice toward freedom. However, what is freeing in the choice of poverty?

Clare's ideal of poverty leads to liberation from the oppression and concern which are inherent in the excessive hoarding of material possessions. Hers is the freedom to share all and everything because creation is abundant and supplies more than enough for all. It encourages living a peaceful and unpretentious existence. Unlike violence, her brand of poverty advertises 'no-power-over-anything-and-anyone.' Avarice and greed are unacceptable alternatives. I believe the '60's Flower children would have found solace in Clare. That movement flowed into the mainstream of American society and became invisible as its proponents aged. On the other hand, Clare's mode of living poverty endures today in some 15,000 Poor Clares throughout the world who practice her enclosed, God-centered, and prayerful model of religious life. What made this possible? I believe it to be Clare's single-hearted focus on poverty's right to live among people, without itself being a subject to violent oppression and threats of annihilation. Essential to its continuation is also an understanding of her view of poverty within the context of her love for and trust in God's Providence. The long Catholic religious tradition, based upon the Gospel Myth of Jesus Christ and itself a survivor in the swirling annals of post-Christian history, also plays a major role in its historic continuation.

The nature of Clare's poverty is in a movement toward freedom, not the glorification of pauperism. Although important to her as food is to survival, poverty nonetheless was neither her reason nor her inspiration for being. These rested in her love relationship to Jesus Christ and Francis, her sisters, and the universe. Clare Offreduccio lived on love. She swallowed love, and love absorbed her even as she absorbed it. However, the scent of poverty played a major role.

A Playful Ode to the Stunts of Odors
Oh, Odors.
Sometimes sweet and sometimes not.
You wander through the tiny slots in noses,
long or pert.
You travel routes both long and short,
from far off barn or city.
You mark the marshland's wild expanse
with musty whiff of geese's' leavings,
left to mold in watery mud,
through winter's bone-chill ev'nings.

When smog congeals, and clogs the nose
in clots of burning smother,
you warn of life-breath taking flight,
and coax all to discover the healing scent of spring's
new day,
in mountains high and ocean's play.

Ah, Odors!
What more be said of your meanderings
through atmospheres diverse?

In acrid smell you bode descent to realms corrupt and
putrid.
In aromas familiar you water the mouth
before palette discovers the morsel.

Baffler, deceiver, you play with the mind
that first sniffs you present in memory's lane,
then you dance away in a swirl of zephyr,
content to leave answers for the breather to find.
Oh Odors!
You stink of garbage and
smell of gardenias,
carry dust to the nose on soft summer breeze causing
exhale of germs in mighty sneeze.
Can anyone harness your dancing power,
Know what to expect with one whiff of your wafting,
Or live friendly with you as companion true?

Enough for now!
I scent the smell of a simmering stew.

BF

The Opening to Love: Union

Poverty is one partner in a union which can be
described as a marriage. Love is the other partner. A
primary union which occurred between Clare and Francis
of Assisi was the wedding of poverty to love. Theirs was a
shared commitment to the Divine and the human, that is to
say, to Jesus Christ and to Lady Poverty. What does this
commitment look like?

Without love, poverty is simply abnegation or, at its
worst, pauperism. As a way of life it is scorned, and it
seems to me from a human point of view, understandably

so. Clare and Francis' own understanding of poverty was couched in the chaos of a feudal social structure which feared and hated poverty. It was considered an evil to be avoided even at the cost of personal integrity. Furthermore, the shift in attitude from dependence upon a feudal system to the independence and interdependence of a mercantile class carried a renewed energy for the poor. They aimed to better their condition and claim their share of the life enjoyed by the nobility. To move toward poverty must have appeared insane from their point of view. To them it likely seemed to be a step backward. Therefore, why would a young and beautiful noblewoman and the son of a prominent and wealthy merchant choose the way of poverty? Every common- sense argument stands in the face of this choice, and brings the onlooker to a chasm of confusion. It is this breech which love bridges. Only love brings light to the underside of poverty, and in the scenario written by Clare and Francis, poverty is the shadow side of love. One without the other negates both as being experiences within the human body and psyche. Poverty and love are flip sides of the same coin in the game of life, dependent upon one another for total identification of each. Nature shows the same dependencies.

Earth teaches the lessons of dependence and interdependence. The moon remains in shadows without the light of the sun. Gravity, holding creation in the embrace of Mother Earth, owes its life to the movement of the moon. There is no day without night. Like the dark side of the moon, the human psyche knows the shadow of suffering in love.

Literature consistently reiterates the theme of love's dance between ecstasy and suffering. Love breaks into the heart. Prose and poetry overflow with tales of love found, lost, and found again; all this in company with pain and joy. An excerpt from a poem by Rumi entitled "Three Quatrains," describes the poet's experience of this alchemical mixture of love and pain:

A night full of talking that hurts, my worst held back secrets:

Everything has to do with loving and not loving. (Barks 313)

Rumi's "talking that hurts" is the language of love. To Shakespeare's Hamlet the question is "to be or not to be." To the poet Rumi it is "to love or not to love." Being has its pain, as Hamlet knew, and love has its hurt as well. Perhaps they are the same question.

Michael J. Meade, one of three editors of the poetry anthology, *The Rag and Bone Shop of the Heart,* suggests in his introduction that when one is reading poetry the listeners' and readers' usual ways of seeing may drop away. In choosing the entry "Three Quatrains," Meade quoted the preceding excerpt from Rumi's poetry to introduce the chapter of the anthology entitled "Earthly Love." The selection takes the reader to new inner places of "loving and not loving," where words pry the heart open to an experience of abandonment in which "Once we surrender, earth surrounds and claims our bodies." Within that surrender, Meade comments that, "We become part of the sensual intimacy of the surprising earth." In other words, sight, touch, and smell are the soil in which humanity roots and out of which it grows. Body weds spirit in an equal partnership where earth meets and consorts with humankind in order that the human race may live through its cycles of evolution into itself. Clare and Francis are wrapped in the activity of the ongoing evolution in the understanding of poverty's place in society. Seeing through the apparent destitution of poverty, they recognized "The Lady Poverty" whose relationship spiraled them out from the realms of desire and love into the experiences of confusion and chaos. In order to better understand this dynamic love, attention is now turned toward how they saw the noble Lady Poverty.

One view of poverty rises from out of an early writing entitled "The Sacred Exchange between Saint Francis and Lady Poverty." The work is included in Volume 1 of a three-volume body of works focused on Francis, who is envisioned respectively in Volume I as "The Saint," Volume II as "The Founder," and Volume III as "The Prophet." In the words of the editorial introduction, "The Sacred Exchange between Saint Francis and Lady Poverty," "is one of the richest texts of the early Franciscan movement... An allegory offering insights into Francis's vision of poverty..." Clare and Francis share in this vision; therefore what is said of Francis within the succeeding pages, can be said of Clare, and vice versa. Furthermore, the mythological will be emphasized over the rational, although not entirely exclusive of it. Nonetheless, the logic of the mind will serve the logic of the heart. We will walk with mythology, literature, and stories in hopes of finding where the scent of poverty, as surrender, opens the mouth of love, as ecstasy. The first considerations will circle around when "The Sacred Exchange between St. Francis and Lady Poverty" was written, and a history of what academic research has already attempted on its behalf.

Scholars Search for the Lady

There is disagreement among the scholars in Franciscan studies concerning the date and authorship of "The Sacred Exchange between Saint Francis and Lady

Poverty." According to the editors of *St. Francis, The Saint,* the composition has been dated at 1227, and credited to the authorship of Thomas of Celano, who wrote three lives of St. Francis. However, the modern day scholarship offers a diversity of possibilities for both the dating and the authorship.

The scholar Stefano Brufani comes to no conclusion in his research as to the exact dating of the manuscript based upon his intense study of thirteen manuscripts, seven of which ended with a statement that states the writing to have been done in 1227. However, judging from the sophistication of the theological thought within its text, Brufani suggests that the disagreements seethed among scholars at the University of Paris between the 1250s and the 1270s. The mendicant life and its choice of poverty were at the heart of this controversy, adding credence to his theory. Furthermore, an issue was made of the fact that Franciscans identified the world as being their cloister, a proclamation which stood in the face of a traditional view that deemed the world to be a soiled and impure place from which a person must withdraw in order to be close to God. This belief reinforced the enclosure of women and the separation of religious people from the secular world around them. These issues may have led to writing a defense of poverty which "The Sacred Exchange" appears to incorporate into its text. In this aspect, the work does show itself to be a defense of poverty as Brufani suggests, and may have resulted from the ongoing controversies taking place at the University of Paris.

Another interpretation of the allegory accents that it might be an indictment of friars who were not living in a manner suited to the poverty which they claimed to espouse. In this view, this allegory is self-interpretive, containing within its context Lady Poverty's own criticism of those who had abandoned and reviled her in the names of forbearance and practicality. She articulates her displeasure or pleasure with clearly described behaviors.

Albeit that the controversies about the time and author of the allegory are important from an historic and academic point of view, enough is said for the sake of background. Since Brufani and other scholars have been unable thus far to determine and agree upon an exact date and author of the work, the years suggested in the text from which the allegory is taken remain the preferred supposed dates. Therefore, for our purposes we will use the dates printed on the introductory page within Volume I, *The Saint*, which are the years between 1237-1239. As to who wrote "The Sacred Exchange between Saint Francis and Lady Poverty," the scholar Placid Hermann simply states that the author is a Franciscan of unknown identity. Franciscan scholars admit that more study and research is needed before concluding date and author. That being what it may, there is a place in mythological studies for further research into this dreamlike masterpiece. The discipline of depth psychology offers first glimpses into a look at where this allegory fits into the fabric of the medieval mind from which it takes its life.

David Bona develops the topic of "The History of Western Dream Theory Interpretation" in Chapter 2 of his 1996 dissertation entitled *The Dreams of St. Francis of Assisi: A Depth Psychological Study*. Bona traces a history of Western dream interpretation from the biblical times, through the Early Church Fathers, and into the Medieval period. In the Old Testament Biblical era, Bona points out that although not the only mode of divine and human exchange, "Dreams and visions, however, are God's primary means of communication"(35). He further explains that according to the Israelites, dreams came from God and their clarification is left either to the dreamer or to the interpretation offered within the context of the dream itself. Bona states:

"For the ancient Israelite, the dream itself contained the interpretation. The interpreter was God, who enlightened the dreamer to its meaning. This premise, central to 13th century dream mentality, is evidenced by those who interpreted St. Francis's dreams. Although valid and important, the premise that God is the interpreter of dreams led to a strictly spiritual interpretation of Francis's dreams, which were clothed almost exclusively in medieval Christian theology and spirituality." (36)

The medieval dreamer, enculturated to perceive God to be the clarifier of dreams, would likely follow the same thought pattern into ferreting out the meaning in an allegory like "The Sacred Exchange." Couching their God within the medieval Church's set of moral standards would lead the reader or listener to conclude that the Lady's descriptions of the negligent and abusive behaviors of the friars toward her are lessons in the good and evil manners of living the vow of poverty. If this be so, then "The Sacred Exchange" becomes a moral tale with an intent to teach and/or admonish.

Bona clearly makes a distinction between his approach to the interpretation of Francis's dreams as viewed from a modern depth psychological perspective and the theological and spiritual perspectives of the medieval times. In making this distinction, Bona finds a new way of viewing the human Francis and opens the topic to ongoing scholarly research.

Following Bona's line of thought, though not his emphasis on depth psychology, the succeeding interpretation of "The Sacred Exchange" will be investigated from a mythological rather than a medieval understanding of dreams and visions. Therefore, the story will be left to unfold as a tale which expresses the complex human struggle to come to grips with human irrational external behaviors and unexplainable internal passions. The clothing of the 'medieval Christian theology' will be stripped away in order to find the underlying themes which are understandable beyond the limits of a specific culture and a particular time. That a dream and/or vision may come from the monotheistic God is left to the belief system of the individual reader. The following mythological approach may include some medieval spirituality, but not necessarily. Meaning emerges from the imagination and the reflections of the listener and reader as is mythology's way. Ideally this will allow "The Sacred Exchange" to enter the royal court of mythology. First, let us look at its genre in order to identify its place more clearly in the realm of mythology studies.

In its Prologue, "The Sacred Exchange between Saint Francis and Lady Poverty" is described as an allegory. The definition of allegory according to *Webster's New Collegiate Dictionary,* is "a. the expression by means of symbolic fictional figures and actions of truths or generalizations about human existence" (18). In the light of this definition, I have placed allegory into the broader realm of mythology for three reasons: first, its symbolic representations; second, its imaginal rather than factual mode of writing; third, it contains universal truths developed in story form. Furthermore, this story as a fictional representation stands on its own merits. It carries meaning, and in turn offers itself as a means of ongoing and personal reflection. Although "The Sacred Exchange" belongs to the larger family of mythology, it possesses hagiographical characteristics from which it must be distinguished: those of inspiring and/or moralizing. Strictly speaking, a myth intends neither. However, it may be used by the listener and reader to enlighten their understanding through discovering meaning within the story. Furthermore, "The Sacred Exchange" may be read from diverse points of view: as an expression of how a Franciscan must live the promise of poverty; or as a call to live the ideal of the virtue; or as a story written in praise of poverty; or as a scolding directed primarily at a lax brotherhood grown cold. The following study will follow none of these interpretations. In the first chapters of this dissertation, I emphasized that a myth does not judge or moralize. Therefore, the story will be interpreted through the broader perspective of the lens of mythology, the genre to which, I believe, allegory belongs. Lady Poverty will tell her own story, expressing humanity's love-hate relationship with her, as well as her marriage relationship with the Divine.

Francis Searches for the Lady

This allegory personifies poverty as an abused and misunderstood noble lady who nonetheless claims her exalted position and expects undivided loyalty and love from her friends, whom she rewards with an abundance of peace, wisdom, and joy. It is time to meet her and to tell the story of her union with those who seek her with love.

The story opens with a prologue extolling the exalted place of poverty among the virtues. The writer claims that the Son of God "fell in love with this virtue with a special affection," and "sought, found, and embraced it" (529). Francis, as the main character of this story, is also described as having given himself eagerly to the same venture as the Son of God by "searching for, finding and embracing holy poverty" (530). The partially paraphrased story of his search now begins:

Francis is restless in his love for the Lady Poverty. He seeks to know her and be with her, but he cannot find her. Therefore, he goes in search of her among the city dwellers, and finds that when he speaks of her among the people, they do not know what he is talking about and/or have no desire to know. The wise men, whom he next questions about Lady Poverty's whereabouts, scorn the seeker and the Lady he endeavors to find. Francis is overcome with gratitude that the knowledge and yearning for the noble Lady should be given to a lowly creature like himself.

Upon leaving the city, Francis chances upon two old men in a field. They are sad and weary. The elders report that they have seen the Lady pass by many time accompanied by companions, but that each time she has returned naked and alone on her way back to her mountaintop abode. The men advise that if Francis should attempt the mountain ascent, he ought not do it alone because companions can help one another in the arduous climb. Choosing faithful companions, Francis begins the journey.

Lady Poverty, from her dwelling on the top of the mountain, spies the men racing up the craggy precipice, unencumbered by worldly baggage.

Astounded, the Lady allows them to approach closer while she decides:

"Therefore, I will speak to them about what engages

my heart so that, when staring down at the abyss that lies about them, they do not, like others, have second thoughts about such a climb. I know they cannot take hold of me without my consent..." (533-34)

The raggle-taggle group draws near. Their spokesperson, Francis, extolls her glory and beauty. He explains that they have come to her whom they love, because their leader, the Son of God, had done so. He admires her constancy and loyalty during the times when everyone else abandoned him. Francis honors her steadfast loyalty to the son of God throughout his earthly life because he left the trappings of an all-powerful godship to take on the nature of a human being. The lowly group standing in her august presence desired to give up all as he did, claiming her as their Lady to whom they pledge their love and constant allegiance. The Lady is moved. She responds by telling them her story:

"I was once in the paradise of God, where man was naked. In fact I was in man and was walking with naked man through that entire splendid paradise, fearing nothing, doubting nothing, and suspecting nothing amiss, who... possessing nothing, he belonged entirely to God. (537)

"However, evil in the form of a serpent 'who could not remain in heaven,' counseled the man in deceit, and the unfortunate creature relented to the advice. Immediately the man became ashamed of his nakedness and covered himself with fig leaves. When God came to walk and talk in the cool of the evening as was God's custom, my companion hid himself. Trembling at majesty and splendor, I met God and cried out, 'Do not enter into judgment with your servant because no living being is justified in your sight' (538). God told me to go away for a while and hide myself from the divine wrath. God then called for my companion who came. Asking an explanation for the man's behavior, God heard only excuses and words of blame.

"Deceiving even himself, the man spoke maliciously and refused to admit the error of his decision. Therefore, God sent the man away from the garden, making him and his posterity subject to death. However, in anger tempered with mercy, God gave the man a garment of skin to replace the lost garment of innocence.

"I drew completely away from the man covered by the garment of death skins. He increased his riches, as I wandered the earth finding no one who wanted my company. Then your Son of God came and claimed me for his own. Then returning to his godship, he left me as a pledge to his faithful ones, whom he counsels: possess no silver, gold or money; control nothing and no one; argue with no one over possessions; give more than what is asked of you; not worry over anything; live in the now time; above all, trust completely in the providence of the divine.

"Nonetheless, these counsels were soon forgotten with the passing of the first followers of the Son and the ending of persecutions. Wars and greed, dissentions and sloth grew among the very people who claimed to honor me. Those who were faithful to me were maligned and exiled. They who were to protect me became my worst enemies, claiming me to be filthy and lazy, that I am indiscreet and have no foresight. Not knowing me nor wanting to know me, they were blinded by external appearances and promises of wealth. I said to them that you are persecuting me, without reason. 'Did I ever tell you that my ways and yours would ever agree? Look, it pains me to have seen you.' I was then cast out and abandoned by men. Then God reminded me that if they had not at first accepted me, they would not be wealthy today and that they pretended to love me. Like my first companion they choose to cling to the deceit. Therefore I am not to grieve over them, nor plead on their behalf."

Her story now completed, Lady Poverty advises the group and Francis to beware of spirits that may deceive them. Reminding them that first fervor passes, she further admonishes them to, "Watch that, after the dung of trivia has been placed at your roots, you may be found barren, for then there is nothing else than for an ax to be used upon" (549). The brothers accepted all her words with joy, asking that she be their companion. The Lady acquiesces.

Descending the mountain together, they banquet on the frugal fare of bread and water. The Lady asks to see their convent, upon which the brothers take her to a hill and showing her all the world they could see, say to her, "This, Lady, is our enclosure." In a final message, the Lady expresses her joy at finding a place on earth where she is united "to those who bear the image of Him to Whom I am espoused in heaven." (553).

The story ends with an expression of praise to the Trinity.

"The Sacred Exchange" unfolds as a journey. Unlike the adventures of the hero Odysseus, who sails into his destiny through arduous feats of conquest and war, Francis scales the craggy earth on an uncharted path through the desire for poverty and love for the Lady who symbolizes it. Furthermore, unlike the noble Odysseus, his personal destiny is secondary to finding and serving the Lady Poverty. Although the motive and goal of their travels differ, the mythic theme of the hero's journey remains a constant. "The Sacred Exchange" is the Franciscan's Odyssey. Where is Clare in this journey?

Lady Clare is symbolic of Lady Poverty in the flesh. The love affair between Francis and Clare shines through this allegory in that it symbolizes a noble woman whose champions attempt the impossible for the prize of a smile and/or, as portrayed in Middle Age masterpiece *Parzival,* the enjoyments of her bed. However, Lady Poverty's bed is the shape of a cross hewn for her beloved, the same master to whom Francis professes an allegiance. In other words, Lady Poverty, Clare, and Francis engage in an interchange comprised of allegiance to the same divinity. As Jesus loved poverty, Clare loved Francis. Why is this important?

Previously in my writings, I suggested that the smell of poverty invaded the entire being of Clare. I also stated that it is the development of the concept of poverty into the daily, practical life-experience at San Damiano which exemplified the gift of poverty open to all humankind, not a chosen few. Clare's understanding of simple dependence upon a provident divinity encouraged others to simplify their lives in order to become and accept who they are without the false trappings of external possessions. In the light of her name, which means light and clarity, and of her forty-two years at San Damiano, she is the lady who lit a way which other human beings could follow; the way of surrendering to love through poverty. She is the personification of a poverty reflecting the Lady who described herself as being espoused in heaven to the one in heaven whose image her followers sustain within themselves. Clare's focus is upon love's committed surrender not the ascetic's disciplined divestment; upon free will, not rigid legalism. Regretfully, Church documents and manuscripts give multiple words of accolades to Clare's sanctity, but little remains of her writings which could shed more light on her insights into this marriage of divinity and poverty. Nonetheless, she is the womb in which Francis's ideal of poverty was conceived, and she nurtured that ideal through the storms of its early growing years. Yet, a question remains. Was Francis Bernadone in love with Clare Offreduccio, who birthed his ideal of a life devoid of all earthly possessions? There are other stories in the mythical treasure trove of Franciscan writings which contribute information for coming to an answer, or at least a better understanding, of the quality of the love between them.

An Ever-present Absence

Absence connotes presence; presence connotes absence. They are consequential to one another. I learned this as a younger woman struggling to discover if I was in love with a man who professed love for me and asked me to marry him. Unsure that I wanted to marry him, I asked my father about how he knew he loved my mother. After some hesitation, he said, "I don't know. It's just that somehow she was always there." When mom died, he deeply suffered her loss. Yet he acknowledged that he also experienced her closeness even after her death. The immediate proximity of my mother took on a more pervasive presence than when she was in the body. It might be said that she was absently present to my father. Had her presence not been known, her absence would never have not been felt.

Georges Bataille offers reflections on the theme of presence-in-absence in *The Absence of Myth: Writings on Surrealism.* In his thoughts, absence takes on an expandability which penetrates the boundaries of the senses. Bataille postulates:

"Perhaps the absence of myth is the ground that seems

so stable beneath my feet, yet gives way without warning. The *absence of God* is no longer a closure: it is the opening up to the infinite. The absence of God is greater, and more divine than God (in the process I am no longer myself, but an absence of self; I await the sleight of hand that renders me immeasurably joyful). And today, because a myth is dead or dying, we see through it more easily than if it were alive: it is the need that perfects the transparency, the suffering which makes the suffering become joyful." (48)

The absence of the object/subject of love, like Bataille's absence of God and myth, opens the need that "perfects the transparency" by way of longing. Self dissolves into the longing which carries the lover from the ecstasy of union to the agony of separation. Consumed by longing, love's desire breaks through the confinement of space and time into that suffering which makes the suffering joyful. There is evidence of this experience of longing being a quality in the human love between Francis Bernadone and Clare Offreduccio. Two stories follow which shed light on this aspect of their love.

One story reports that Francis stripped himself in the middle of winter, went out into the freezing cold, and sculpted himself a wife and children from the snow accumulated on the ground. Then he rolled and rolled naked in the snow. Was this the action of a madman or a man madly in love? Does this exceptional and extravagant behavior rise from the head of his body or the head of his penis? Perhaps both. Perhaps Francis responded to his sexual heat by externalizing it in its oppositional balance of the ice cold snow, his own version of a cold shower. Burning desire for sexual intimacy, a wife, and progeny were likely no strangers to this very human and passionate man.

One story of Clare's experience of an earthy expression of human love includes a vision which Clare reported to one of her sisters. It is included in the records of her canonization process and also in the book, *Clare of Assisi: Early Documents,* edited by Regis Armstrong. In it the third witness, Sister Filippa, relates that she was told of a vision in which Clare brought a towel and bowl of hot water to Francis. She was effortlessly ascending a high stairway, and upon reaching Francis, he bared his breast to her and said, "Come, take and drink." After she had sucked from the breast, the saint told her to drink again. Upon drinking a second time, Clare describes the taste as sweet and delightful. The words in the process continue:

"After she had imbibed, that nipple or opening of the breast from which the milk came remained between the lips of blessed Clare. After she took what remained in her mouth in her hands, it seemed to her it was gold so clear and bright that everything was seen in it as in a mirror." (144)

What can be made of this extraordinary fleshly portrayal of human nurturing? What does it say to us of the love relationship between Clare and Francis? First it exhibits a marked sexual maturity which reversed the accepted cultural roles of the man and woman, even to the bodily manifestation of feeding at the breast of the masculine Francis. "The Sacred Exchange" pictures Francis's search as parallel to that portrayed in the 'Song of Songs' of the Hebrew *Tanakh* (1405-1424). He becomes the "black but beautiful" Shulamite woman who begins the search for the Beloved by questioning the people who might have the information, but like her, finds that they cannot or will not help. Francis not only incorporates a woman's journey into a man's odyssey, but he travels the feminine route of love's desire rather than a more masculine hero's quest to reach his destiny. There is an androgynous quality which likely carried over in the external relationship between Clare and Francis. Clare's vision shows evidence of this gender exchange and its alchemical quality.

Clare suckles at the breast of the man Francis, tasting a milk too sweet to describe. The nipple from which the milk flowed stays on her lips. Her mouth holds that which becomes gold when placed in her hands. Seen from the perspective of alchemy as elucidated by Edward Edinger in *Anatomy of the Psyche*, "The alchemical *opus* was considered a process begun by nature but requiring the conscious art and effort of a human being to complete." Edinger continues by quoting from *The Lives of the Alchemystical Philosophers* that, "This state [the *opus*] cannot be perfected by the mere progress of nature; for gold has no propensity to move itself so far; but rather chooses to remain in its constantly abiding body" (8). I suggest that had the gold of Francis's ideal not been taken in by Clare, the practical possibility of living it within the context of human experience would have been severely handicapped. A strict adherence to only one way of living poverty in surrender to providence left no opening for the ideal to move from the mind and heart of Francis into the minds and hearts of a broader humanity. More important, it may have remained in the realm of idealism packed away in church annals, had Clare not expended forty-two years of effort and perseverance in order to complete the work of securing the future of Lady Poverty under the auspices of the widespread tradition of Catholicism. Furthermore, her community proved that the ideal could be lived. The official acceptance of her Form of Life was the ultimate expression of the completion of the work. However, the characteristic personified specifically in Clare's vision is that of the earthly human experience of suckling at the breast, specifically a woman's task based upon her anatomy. The exchange of gender roles is clear in these stories. Clare and Francis remain unique in their sexuality, but united in their gender; that is to say, they hold to their physicality as manifested in masculine and feminine body parts, but do not fall into the abstract classification of those traits as defined and declared by grammatical and cultural expectations. There is nothing abstract about their love. It is down and dirty, meaning earthy. There is yet another story which signifies a strength of presence experienced in absence, as shown in the previous dreams and visions.

One added comment: let it be noted that this allegory incorporates a different story of the "fall" of Adam and Eve as told in the biblical text. As is mythology's task, it changes the contents of the story without changing its basic truth. One might call this the story of the Fall from the Franciscan perspective.

She is always Here

Western Franciscan scholars focus their efforts on discovering, translating, and researching recent and past manuscripts, investigating them from theological, historical, and spiritual points of view. This is done in order to better understand the Franciscan charism. Mythology is not their primary concern, although it is always there hidden away in the human story. Nonetheless recent scholarship has contributed treasure troves of translated materials abundant with legends and stories waiting to be mined. The two last volumes of a collection of manuscripts unearthed and translated into English within the years

1999-2001, and respectively entitled, *Francis of Assisi, The Founder,* and *Francis of Assisi, The Prophet,* contain material which I believe comprises a uniquely Franciscan mythology. It awaits investigation from a mythological point of view. However, it is presently the main concern of this dissertation to point its mythological camera in the direction of one legend which enlightens the quality of the love relationship between Clare and Francis. It holds its place in the eight-hundred-year-old tradition, or later interpretations of that tradition. The story comes from a collection entitled *The Little Flowers of Saint Clare* written by Piero Bargellini and translated by Edmund L'Gorman, O.F.M.Conv. It will serve to underscore the absence-presence motif within the love between Clare and Francis. Following is a summary which recounts the legend entitled "The Face in the Well":

After a visit to the convent of the Poor Ladies, Clare, moved by a greater desire to remain strong in her love for God, multiplied her prayer and penance. Francis, at a far distance from the convent, was praying at night. He prayed that the Poor Ladies would shine as brilliant as the night skies, but the skies were silent in confirming that his prayer was heard. He was to look down rather than up for that assurance.

On a night when the moon shone full, he and Brother Leo arrived at an open well. Francis approached it, and stood in deep stillness peering down into its depths. They then continued on the journey, Francis not having had a drink of the water and nonetheless in the state of ecstatic joy. Feeling the perplexity of his companion Francis explained that he saw in the well the face of "our Sister Clare" whom he thought was suffering and under temptation. Instead, she was all peace and brightness. Francis's heart was then set at peace concerning Clare and he gave thanks to God, saying, "After God and His heavens - Clare!"

Clare precedes the brothers in Francis's hierarchy of importance in this myth. It has been noted that Francis made a point of leaving his assurance that the brothers would always be solicitous for the Ladies. Although Franciscan history reports that this commitment was not always upheld by the men, it is recorded for posterity in the document "The Form of Life Given to Saint Clare and Her Sisters" included in the text *Francis and Clare.* Francis pledges, "...I resolve and promise for myself and for my brothers always to have that same loving care and special solicitude for you as [I have] for them" (45). There is no question that Francis cared deeply for Clare and the Sisters. Nonetheless it is Clare who holds a central place in Francis's affection. The three stories summarized above tell of soul mates involved in a close and tender relationship, a relationship inclusive enough to overflow into the lives of their followers, who were included in their love for one another. The following are stories more particular to their relationship with one another.

Affection and the Incarnation of Love
Affect detonates an emotional explosion. According to an entry in the text, *A Critical Dictionary of Jungian Analysis,* the ego becomes captive to the power of a blast of affect. An excerpt from an entry comparing affect and feeling reads:

"One has command over feeling, whereas affect intrudes against one's WILL and can only be repressed with difficulty. An explosion of affect is an invasion of the individual and a temporary takeover of the EGO. Our emotions happen to us. Affect occurs at the point at which our ADAPTATION is the weakest and at the same time exposes the reason for its weakness." (Samuels, Shorter, and Plaut 11)

An analogy of the detonation inherent in the meeting of affect and ego is found in the controlled explosion which powers an automobile's movement. In the automobile's battery, the igniting spark between the positive and negative poles energizes the motor into moving the vehicle. That contained fire, the spark, creates enough havoc to energize an immobile object as big as a car into action. So does affection spark the possibility of a relationship to move the individual beyond the conscious knowledge of oneself. It makes room for new questions, luring one to reflect upon the passing new horizons of unexpected and unplanned explosions of affect.

The most frequent experience of an affective visitation is that of "falling in love." Phrases contain affect without explanations: "their eyes met across a crowded room," "lost in her eyes," "locked in a gaze," "eyed one another," "avoided eye contact." No reports by those who knew her describe Clare as avoiding eye contact as part of her aesthetical practice. On the contrary, she is consistently described as joyful and tender, characteristics conducive to warm and human communication. Clare practices that communication, articulating her affect through her contemplative prayer, various extant writings, and a conscious service to others. These became the means for connecting her bodily emotions to her spiritual experiences. The separation of body and soul were not a part of Clare's spiritual teachings. Furthermore, the division of mind and heart find no place in her understanding of the unity inherent in creation. Clare's articulated simplicity is eloquently concise in the three words which embrace her entire form of contemplation, one in which the eyes play a major role: Look- Gaze-Place Yourself. She demands no particular positioning of the body, no breathing-in and breathing-out exercises, no sound or words to connect one to the universe, no advice not to allow thoughts or images to enter the mind, and most revealing, no direct warnings to avoid distractions at prayer. Her concern was far from physical and mental self-disciplines. She simply advised that nothing and no one be allowed to turn the gaze away from love and attention to the beloved Divine. Her words focus on being present to life here and now. A free woman herself, Clare left it to each sister to connect with her unique humanness and to cherish affect as a means to effect transformation. Focus lighted upon the daily occurrences of life where kindness, courtesy, and affection were expected. The heart of this focus is summarized in Bill Moyer's collection of interviews with Joseph Campbell entitled *The Power of Myth*. Chapter 7, "Tales of Love and Marriage", opens with a poem from a twelfth century poet, Guiraut de Borneilh. His word images resonate with Clare's union of body and spirit. Seeding love by the meeting of eyes, de Borneilh writes:

> So through the eyes love attains the heart:
> For the eyes are scouts of the heart,
> And the eyes go reconnoitering
> For what it would please the heart to possess.
> And when they are in full accord
> And firm, all three, in the one resolve,
> At that time, perfect love is born

From what the eyes have made welcome to the heart.
Not otherwise can love either be born or have commencement
Than by this birth and commencement moved by inclination.

By the grace and by command
Of these three, and from their pleasure,
Love is born, who its fair hope
Goes comforting her friends.
For as all true lovers
Know, love is perfect kindness,
Which is born - there is no doubt - from the heart and eyes.
The eyes make it blossom; the heart matures it:
Love, which is the fruit of their very seed.

Campbell credits the twelfth century troubadours with birthing the present day's sense that love entails a uniquely person-to-person relationship. The interview goes on to explore the transformation of the love ideal from the impersonal to the personal within the history of Western Europe. Enhanced by the introduction of Eastern philosophy and wealth brought back with the soldiers returning from the Crusades, and the opening of new trade routes to the East, love expanded with the human psyche beyond the confines of the impersonal loves known as Agape and Eros. Eros transformed into Amor, whose arrows carry a pointed and personal experience of the wound of love. Unlike the all-inclusive impulse of Agape love, Amor is felt as "a total physiological and psychological explosion." Campbell also says that it was the troubadours who changed the perception of love as a solely sexual urge to a power which penetrates deeply into the human heart and mind. As Campbell attests, "The troubadours recognized Amor as the highest spiritual experience" (186). It stands to reason that, being children of the late twelfth and early thirteenth centuries, Clare and Francis inherited this mental shift. That the troubadours made their mark in the psyche of young Francis is evidenced in the story of his roaming the woods surrounding Assisi singing love songs at the top of his voice, and using two sticks to symbolize a violin-like musical instrument. This behavior exemplifies a decided incorporation of affectivity into his style of loving, just as Clare's choice of affectionate speech in her letters displays hers. They embodied their spirituality in a particular mode of externalization.

Edward C. Whitmont in *The Symbolic Quest* deals with the interplay of emotion and feeling. He stresses the union of the dualities of positive and negative, feelings and emotions, inferior and superior functions, and aggressive and warm sensitive responses:

"By paying attention to unpredictable reactions one can discover what one's real emotions happen to be, regardless of will and intent. Such awareness transforms blind emotions into genuine feelings, opens the doors to the soul, to the integration of spontaneity, sensitivity, receptivity, adaptability and warmth, but also to the assimilation of aggressiveness and the inferior functions, hence of the ability to direct one's temper constructively."

The fruits of Clare and Francis's relationship leave little doubt that the affective quality plays a major role in the form and style of their spirituality. It lives in the documents written by their own hands. The continuous affirmative response on the part of countless individuals who have chosen to follow them for eight hundred years tells of an ideal which strums the heartstrings of the human heart, where memory is at its most intense and unpredictable. Although they were intelligent, intellectuality dissolves in the heat of their passionate involvement in their own lives and those of others. I believe that the affective character of their relationship is their unique gift to the broader human story of love, carrying love into a deeper understanding of its own desire for union.

Resting genuinely in a human response to an inner light, it just so happened in history that the same light was seen by a woman and man whose primary love for the divine carried them into deeply felt love for one another. Stories, chosen from among many others, are meant to offer insights into the affective and emotional nature of friendship between Clare and Francis. They couch intimacy in the bodily feelings and actions of washing, nursing, sleeplessness for worry over a loved one's welfare, and joy over knowing all is well. The stories exemplify a psychic connection between the two, with emphasis on a particular aspect of their humanity, that of loving affection.

Was genital intimacy part of their affective relationship with one another?

It is this writer's belief that it is unlikely that their relationship included genital intimacy. This view is based upon the personal integrity which they exhibited, and which was attested to by those who knew them throughout their lives. If they had been intimate, they would have admitted it. Up to the time of this writing, no research has uncovered hard evidence to back up a theory of physical union between them. That is not to say that the physical manifestation of love is wrong or bad. It just does not seem likely to have been part of their relationship. The many reports of those who knew them attest to the fact that Clare and Francis always met with others present. Furthermore, the code of personal discipline consistently exercised by Clare and Francis in all other areas of their spiritual and physical practice does not suggest that they would bed down with one another. I believe that Clare and Francis of Assisi were partners in the commitment and desire to be one with the divine, and were united in a bond of mutual affection and friendship with each other deep enough to enter one another's psyche. However, there is no academic or historical evidence. Although their possible sexual relationship may be of interest in the context of the modern focus on the place of sexual intimacy in a healthy human relationship, pursuing this path offers no further enlightenment on an understanding of the relationship between Clare and Francis.

From a mythological point of view, Psyche and Amor are active participants in the Clare and Francis love story. The journey took them on an inner adventure together, which they shared as separate individuals. A remarkable feat indeed. That they shared the same theological underpinnings makes the story more astonishing, since the church of their day remained a staunch divider of body and soul, spirit and matter, and feminine and masculine.

Did Clare love Francis? Did Francis love Clare? Were they "in" love with one another? Yes, on all counts. Without violating the outgoing character of a love based upon a commonly held ideal of another Beloved, who was beyond and yet in the midst of their love for one another, they maintained a commitment to their separate and communal calls. Their relationship encompassed being sexual and being human.

A final story on the topic of unity-in-love holds a fit description of an inimitably feminine response to the machinations of love between woman and man. It is from the collection *The Little Flowers of St. Clare* and is simply entitled "The Roses." The story begins with an explanation of Clare's earlier years at San Damiano when she needed the affirmation and guidance of Francis in her new communal life. She requested that Francis visit more frequently and that the visits might entail more than his usual stopping at the door to wish the sisters peace and then being on his way. The story continues:

"One cold winter's day Francis stood, ready to leave, as he had come, without having accepted any other comfort than the knowledge that true poverty was being observed and that all the young nuns were happy in their life. So he walked toward the door. Outside the wind whistled and blew through the branches of the olive trees, and snow was settling in little droves and sleet was forming upon the front pathway. Francis' bare feet stepped out into the snow and Clare followed after him a few paces away. She hoped to detain him a little. At least she hoped to get a promise from him of another visit soon.

Francis pulled his hood up over his head:

'Sister Clare', he said, 'it is better that we go our own ways, because of what the world might think. I will leave you to manage on your own.'

Clare, standing in the brightness of the ground, felt lost and astray:

'What will I do without you? You are my guide and support.'

Francis raised his eyes to the somber sky:

'Our Blessed Lord will guide you.'

'And we will not see you again?'

Francis looked about. Considering the weather conditions and seeing a thorny rosebush covered with snow, he said to Clare:

'We will meet again when the roses reflower.'

It was the beginning of winter, and the roses would not flower again until well into the spring. He wanted to place a complete season between himself and Clare.

'Let it be as you wish', answered Clare, 'but also as Our Lord wishes'. And she bowed her head.

Francis made a move away, but almost immediately he involuntarily stopped. On the bush that was near him suddenly and miraculously groups of roses had flowered!

Clare, under her double veil... smiled to herself." (Bargellini 66-68)

The meaning of this story, like all good myths, is left to the interpretation of the reader. I interpret Clare's smile as being that matchless expression of a woman who has obtained the desire of her heart without force or argumentation. She disarmed her beloved friend by the sheer use of her wits, and by accessing the very source from which their mutual love emerged. While Francis insisted upon moving away, Clare persisted in moving toward. This dynamic seems to possess an inherent quality of love: sometimes going toward, sometimes running from, however always present to the other even in absence. It was no different with Clare and Francis. Clare's love for Francis stretched through forty-two years of his presence and absence. Without it, there would be no Clare as she is known and portrayed in history, and there would be no Francis as he is remembered and revered. As for the innumerable little Franciscan children streaming through the annals of history, they show that the fertility of the divinities continues to defy the limits of time, the confines of culture, and the boundaries of the physical body.

> *A Love Affair*
> Human,
> longing to behold the face of Love stolen in a moment
> of ecstatic gaze.
> Divinity,
> yearning to embrace human beauty
> in flames of fiery consummation.
> Divinely human, Humanly divine.
> One in the gaze and one in the hiding,
> both fleeing the other,
> yet wanting to be found,
> Fearing to disintegrate at their meeting
> in one fleeting moment of exploding fire.
> Lost in time, to love forever.
>
> BF

Chapter Five
Summary

The goal of this dissertation was primarily to get to know the thirteenth-century woman, Clare Offreduccio of Assisi, who founded a community of nuns who practiced poverty as promulgated by St. Francis of Assisi, and who is considered the first woman Franciscan. The second goal was to discover what this eight-hundred-year-old woman has to say to people of the twenty-first century.

The study began with a vision, which was viewed in the Jungian sense of vision as "an eruption of an unconscious content which intrudes upon the field of consciousness in the form of an impressive experience" and is "portrayed in visual and pictorial terms" (Samuels, Shorter, Plaut 159). While I sat slumped in an overstuffed chair at a local coffee shop, I was visited by the vision of a woman dressed in a tee shirt and blue jeans, hair drawn back and left leg slung over the arm rest of an easy chair opposite mine. The visionary figure became a living symbol who invaded my psyche and would not be dismissed from that day on. This first meeting at the coffee shop evolved into the topic for this dissertation. The woman in blue jeans wanted a voice through which to speak; the encounter with her led me to decide to study and write about her. In this endeavor, I hoped both to listen to and to speak her story. The woman identified herself as "Clare."

Because I had been in the Franciscan sisterhood for almost fifty years, the name Clare led me to think of the woman who partnered Francis of Assisi in the founding of religious orders of nuns, sisters, and brothers in the thirteenth century. The only image I had of her at the time was as a nun shrouded in reams of coarse cloth, with head veiled, and feet bared, gazing outward through very tired eyes. Clare entered into the early years of our religious formation as the holy shadowy, but not quite human, woman follower of Francis; not as the co-foundress of the Franciscan way, as I now consider her to be. I wanted to know and understand how and why she was lost in shadows of history. What of her story was not being told? What does she say for herself? However, I wondered how to go about exhuming a woman wrapped in shadows and buried in eight hundred years of history.

Mythological in Approach, Method and Style

The intellectual discipline of mythological studies opened one route into solving the dilemma of finding a way into studying Clare. I chose to travel where that avenue might lead. The challenge was to bring literature, history, and depth psychology into the service of mythology. I chose to make use of these other scholarly approaches to enhance and support mythology as the principle academic lens through which Clare would be studied. Early in the writing, I saw that my investigations lacked two advantages afforded to the study of many other historical figures: first, the technological advances in news and television coverage, which allow for a more immediate communication of the lives, deeds, and contributions to the public sector of modern persons; second, the multitude of documents and manuscripts available to those who wish to research many figures, especially male figures, of the distant past.

Clare's mark on history is not testified to in a documentary film based upon the immediate experience of her in modern times. As for the lack of written documentation, only in recent years have scholars in Franciscan studies discovered some relevant documents and letters from European convents and church archives. However, Clare's few extant writings are limited in scope and number. Those most useful to this dissertation included Four Letters to Agnes of Prague, the Testament, Clare's Form of Life or Rule, and her Blessing. In addition to these is the *Process of Canonization*. Although the latter was not written by her, it became an invaluable resource for information about Clare's enclosed life at her convent of San Damiano, and her personal relationships with those who knew her over her entire life span. The aforementioned documents are but a few sources which described the convent order of the day, gave information about her early life at home, and testified to her influence on the Church and the feudal society of her day. Furthermore, these served to reinforce deeper understandings of the legends and myths surrounding Clare.

Added to the hurdles of limited documentation is the fact that the honed imaginative talent of the twelfth and thirteenth centuries used stories for education, information, inspiration, and moral formation, which makes these sources far from objective, neutral, and historical reportage according to today's understandings. To base a dissertation on such stories does not easily fit the predominant academic emphasis on the empirical and rational scholarship. However, I believed that an academic study which looks at such material mythologically could incorporate the perspectives of other academic disciplines and issue in a new understanding of the stories and legends surrounding Clare. That is what I set out to do, and a human Clare emerged as a woman whose ideas and practices fit well into the today's world, particularly in the area of leadership and self-determination.

I wrote my way through this dissertation and came to understand why Clare of Assisi is not remembered in this century for her personal accomplishments. It is true that she is portrayed as a saint who is a model of perfection, as I point out in a comparison between hagiographies. However the hagiography embellishes her character so that the ordinary eyes of ordinary people cannot penetrate through and into the fullness of Clare's human nature. Furthermore, an appreciation of her down-to-earth actions is minimized by the unusual emphasis placed upon those situations which were considered to be extraordinary or miraculous. The ordinary beauty of her daily life and relationships remained in the dark. I wonder what Clare's mother, Ortulana, would answer to the request, "Tell us about your daughter. What was she like?" In response, (at least in the early days of her daughter's life at San Damiano) she may be able to empathize with the mother of a Simone Weil. Weil's twentieth-century mother must have struggled to understand the strange things her daughter did for apparently good reasons. What were her thoughts as her daughter almost starved herself to death in order to demonstrate her compassion for those who go hungry because of the unjust distribution of land and money? The point is that historical facts concerning the life and activities of Simon Weil remain in the human conscious memory pool, whereas remembrance of Clare of Assisi inhabits deeper waters of the collective psyche. Therefore knowledge of the human Clare needed either fishing out or diving deeper. The vessels for this exploration were legends and stories. The *Process of Canonization,* The Testament, Rule, and Letters, and studies by other scholars contained matter which under the scrutiny of history, depth psychology, and literature offered valuable insights into her character. Nonetheless, the genuine characteristics of her personality emerge most effectively in her legends, which are much more like stories shared at the wakes of those who have died and live on in the memories of people who have experienced them in everyday life. The stories are vignettes of the true personality. The legends of Clare hold the endearing qualities which underline the meaning of her relationships, and give glimpses into her war-blooded humanness.

This study begins with a comparison of hagiography and mythology in order to clarify my choice of myth as a preferred story form. Hagiography tends toward being didactic, inspirational, and moralizing. Myth tells the story and allows its meaning to be unraveled by the reader or listener in the light of history, culture, and the search for answers to questions that have accompanied humankind throughout the ages: How did life begin? Who are we? Where did we come from? Where are we going? Why do we suffer? Why does love hurt? What is the source of evil and good? What happens when we die? What might this story mean for us at this time in history?

Mythology claims center stage in this study because its dimensions include the writer of the story, the director, the players, and the audience. No one is left out. Mythology is the universal tale of humanity wrapped in the story-skins of each human being. Furthermore, the contributions of depth psychology helped me to discover a new view of Clare by means of active imagination, dreams, legends, literature, and visions. J. Marvin Spiegelman's psycho-mythology, which takes Jung's concept of active imagination into deeper realms of individual transformation, was to be one of the means by which I would connect to the psyche of Clare as manifested in my vision of her as the woman in blue jeans.

Clare's Story

I had hoped to keep Francis of Assisi as far out from this study of Clare as possible due to the fact that his overwhelming personality has overshadowed her for hundreds of years. I discovered that Francis as the man in Clare's life could not be avoided. Clare's friendship with Francis influenced her option for a poverty manifested in a total divestment of material possessions and influential prestige. The motivation for her choice was to come to total dependence upon the Love of God in Jesus Christ. Francis influenced Clare's life after her early young womanhood as she did his. The circumstances of their meeting and the vast differences in their economic and social standing serve to demonstrate that their partnership was extraordinary. Within the context of such differences, their personalities could well have clashed. Clare, refined and honest, dislikes the spectacular, and self-centered; Francis, spontaneous and fun-loving, seeking fame and self-gratification. The merchant's son and the nobleman's daughter were an unlikely match in the thirteenth-century social and economic structure. Their paths would seldom cross.

Although they had well-chaperoned, clandestine meetings before Clare ran away from home at age nineteen, they saw one another infrequently after she began her enclosed life at San Damiano. Theirs was a close relationship lived separately from each another. Furthermore, Clare's spirituality was well formed before she chose to leave her home to join Francis. She developed a new style of religious community in which he did not participate. She developed a style of egalitarian community in her own home and brought that to birthing an evolutionary new way of life: a way attested to and practiced in community settings for over eight hundred years. I pursued this study keeping foremost in my mind that there is a Clare exclusive of Francis of Assisi, whose story developed in a manner unique to her personality, and who is a woman with contributions to the broader history of the world and particularly to women's advancement in that history. However, it became evident that a study of Clare entirely exclusive of Francis would eliminate the most human side of Clare's character.

I continued pursuing my acquaintance with a woman who for eight hundred years was not perceived as affecting the course of history, but was remembered as the friend and soul mate of a more overwhelming historic figure. She had been kept alive by a canonization process of the Catholic Church, which put her into the category of a holy virgin, giving no hint that she modeled a form of life in which women had control of their own destiny; much less mention of rigorous attempts to subject her to a Papal Rule of Life which undermined her vision. Perhaps when on her deathbed she was finally presented with the copy of her Rule which held the official signatures needed for Papal approbation, it was expected that it would be buried forever in the grave along with its writer. That was not to be. The Poor Clares' and her Form of Life live on through the ages, albeit through the stormy history of reforms and distortions of her intent. But does the living energy of Clare survive into the twenty-first century?

The present-day Poor Clare nuns survive as a living testimony that Clare founded a way of life which pierces the barriers of time. Nonetheless, Clare remains an enigma to this present age, which emphasizes the importance of the individual, and the right to live out one's unique gifts. Like an image of a "good wife and mother," Clare chose to stay enclosed at San Damiano, hidden in the shadows of convent life and tending her soul, the souls of her sisters, and the physical and spiritual needs of others who sought her help. Self-demeaning as this sounds to the modern woman, a restricted view of women's gifts prevailed in the twelfth and thirteenth centuries although there were some efforts to change that attitude. Men like Joachim de Flora and communities like the Beguines are but two examples. However, socially and historically, Clare was a woman of her times, brought up in a milieu which accepted the suppression of women. She was caught in the same net through which she gnawed an escape for herself and her sisters into a difficult but self-determining existence. Yet the question spurred by this dissertation remained: What does this say to the twenty-first century woman and man? During the writing of the early chapters of the dissertation, it appeared that she might be giving a negative message and clear advice about what not to do or believe.

The writing of Chapter 4 led me on the darkest, and most productive experience of writing. Choosing to work with four characteristics which formed the base of the spiritual and organizational structures upon which Clare built her life, I could say that at this juncture the dissertation and I became friends. The main features of Clare's way of loving were seen as the features of the human senses. The four features I chose to describe Clare's face of love were the "The Eyes of Contemplation: The Gaze"; "The Touch of Community: Leadership"; "The Scent of Poverty: Simplicity"; and "The Mouth of Union:

Consummate Love."

Main Features

"The Eyes of Contemplation" required that if I were to get to Clare's idea of "the gaze", as basic to her spiritual contemplative mode, it was necessary to experience her style of contemplative prayer myself. As pointed out in the first chapter of this work, prayer is a familiar way for me to enter the spiritual realm. Clare became my mentor as she was for Agnes, a younger noblewoman whom Clare guided in founding a convent of Poor Ladies in her native city of Prague. I practiced, in a limited way, what Clare advised Agnes to do when she prayed. I twice daily sat down for twenty minutes before a replica of the cross of San Damiano with nothing else than "Look-Gaze-Place Yourself", and "My God and All." It proffered me little satisfaction in terms of feeling higher or closer to God, for the most part. Now as I reflect upon this practice which has become a daily activity, I ask myself, "What has changed? What have I learned?" Suffice it to say that I no longer think in terms of feeling closer to the Divine, a Higher Power, a Goddess, or any other Energy greater than myself. It is not necessary to my peace of mind, because I know without a doubt that the All, which is known by more names than the entire collective consciousness can conjure, is closer to me than I can imagine whether I feel it or not. Added to this is an assurance that I am just fine being who I am. For one who has striven to be perfect all her life, this new-found confidence brings peace of mind, for the most part. These are simple transformations with huge ramifications on how I live my daily existence in the form of an embodied spirit and inspirited body. Peace of mind is no small thing to call one's own. I accept and know that when Clare described a Presence "whose contemplation refreshes... whose fragrance revives," I know of what she speaks. Can I empirically prove that these changes occurred because I contemplated as Clare suggested? No. I can only say that I did nothing else differently in the other aspects of my life during the time I practiced this style of contemplation which might account for this change of attitude and inner disposition. Also, I know Clare better and want to know more. That too is a change. Have all of the preceding realizations made me more patient? Kind? Considerate? Affectionate? Enlightened? It would be nice; however I neither know nor am concerned about them. All I know is that I like myself better with all my warts and that other people seem somehow more fun, more interesting, and tremendous mysteries. The empirical evidence of such change is in the living. What has happened is that I know myself, my community of sisters, and my approach to everyday life in a clearer, more accepting light. One small indication of transformation is that I have reentered into direct service within my own community through membership on a leadership committee. The goal of the group is to do a two-year study in order to discover new models of leadership more conducive to the ministries and life styles of the twenty-first century sister. It has been time consuming, confrontational and exciting. I recognize a new power within me. As noted in a quotation from Stephen Aizenstadt in the opening chapter of this dissertation, "...Not only does the topic call the person, but the person goes into her own experience and wonders how she is affected by the topic... When the person and the topic come into relation, the other possibilities emerge." And other possibilities did emerge as I continued the study of

Clare based upon main characteristics which shone through as topics to be investigated.

The section "Touch of Community" demanded my waiting-for-the-right-word. Surrender to emotions of anger that welled when considering Clare's mandated enclosure, and the realization that misogynist attitudes prevail in today's Catholic tradition, I channeled my raging energy into focusing on the matter at hand. This was a challenge which included an exaction of flesh, that is to say, that I place my derriere to the chair in the solitude of writing through my own emotions, and into the heart of a woman who gave only glimpses of herself word by word. This led to the irony that Clare's example did not continue as a renewal of life for the women within her own religious Catholic tradition, but became particularized in the form of a diversity of present day Franciscan communities.

Although Clare never aimed at innovating the feudal system or the Church, nor set out to change her society, her vision posed a threat to the organized powers of her day. In a misconstrued understanding of Clare's intent, the political and ecclesial leaders of her day may have feared that if everyone were to live simplicity and generosity, the sources of their wealth and influence would disappear. True. Without the labor of serfs and the liaisons with and among the nobility, the entire base for a secure future evaporates into the thin air of mercantilism and an open-market economy. It needed lands bequeathed by the nobility and the labor of the common people to keep a hold on power and control. Clearly, this was a very different church from the one envisioned by both Clare and Francis. They envisioned a church based on love and mercy, justice and peace. They embraced a universal church existent as a living organism birthed by Christ as a people of God, not a structural organization emanating from the machinations of a controlling few. Clare's life work issued from a living love-connection woven into the fabrics of herself, her higher power, her sisters and brothers, and all of creation. Out of these joint relationship sprang those influences which contributed to the downfall of the feudal system, however, not to the demise of the Ecclesial monarchical structure upon which the Catholic Church is organizationally modeled. That is further attested and examined to by some modern writers.

Leonard Schlain, author of *The Alphabet Versus the Goddess,* traces the relationship between word and image in an historical study of the emergence of the alphabet and the concomitant demise of the feminine principle as symbolized by the goddess. In Chapter 28, "Mystic / Scholastic, 1000--1300", he narrates the dramatic upsurge of women's energy and acceptance in the fields of literature, education,   religion, and business in the early Middle Ages. However by the High Middle Ages, the progress halts and Schlain summarizes what he believes to be the cause. He states:

"As Europe emerged from the Dark Ages, for a time the feminine and the masculine and right and left-brain values came into balance. But as the Church reasserted control, left-brain and masculine values became dominant again, and the gains women had made were lost. The years ahead would bear dramatic witness to the calamity that results when a culture's collective left hemisphere hypertrophies." (308)

Schlain's theory was most emphatically present as I worked the topic of leadership. That Clare's practice of leadership would parallel that of present day entrepreneurial attitudes came as a surprise as I progressed through the writing. Her motivation and goals differed, but the practical, applied, passionate pursuit of those goals was shown to be the same. Clare's intent was spiritual and rested upon equality among the sisters, insistence upon making contemplation the central ministry within their call to San Damiano, encouragement toward their learning to know themselves, and inspiration to remain focused on their passion; the passion being to be caught up in a love affair with God. Clare's concern was that her sisters be on the path of "prudent happiness," so as to live what they loved and love what they lived. That was the "product" she was perfecting and selling.

Her practices were definitely in keeping with modern day encouragement to pursue dreams, work out from your passion, and enjoy the process along the way. This was not the generally accepted attitude of her day. Her goals added the dimension of building a community while improving the product, and the lives of the sisters who were included in communal decision making. Although there is no evidence that she set out to develop a new understanding of leadership, she simply remained faithful to her genius and vision, endeavoring to make them into a shared life reality in community. That was threat enough to the powers that be in her times.

The remembrance of Clare endures, based upon her philosophy and the manner in which she chose to practice her beliefs. She practiced a style of leading which stood in opposition to the authoritative modes of her upbringing and her surrounding society. As attested to in the Process of Canonization, Clare practiced leadership among her sisters and modeled the way of becoming first-among-equals; Clare as Abbess personified a new mode of authority. She rejected the notion of being superior to anyone and exemplified an inclusive spirit, modeling a style of leadership-of-the-many which expected that her sisters to be part of the decision-making process, and not subjects of a higher authority other than the Divine.

As the topical study progressed, it became clear that although Franciscan scholarly research continues to unravel the mystery of Clare's shadowy presence, her contributions rest in what is not said, as well as what is said, both by herself and by the writers of her day. From the viewpoint of contemporary scholarship what is not said is conventionally not open to serious consideration as material for scholarly research. Nonetheless, the mythological approach made it possible for the woman to begin to rise from out of the shadows and absences.

The absence of extended detail in the written document of her Form of Life, known as the Rule by the Catholic Church, left room to imagine life in the community at San Damiano as being one of collegiality and mutual love. The Benedictine Rule, which the Papacy mandated that she follow, contains clear strictures, demands, and punishments on violators. It was not acceptable to Clare, so she wrote her own less wordy text, the first Rule written by a woman for women and approved by the Church. Her staunch rejection of the Rules written by the Church and the Benedictine Rule attest to Clare's clarity of vision and inner assurance of it validity. Her Form of Life offers insight into the woman who wrote it. However, being a formal document, it cannot supply that which marks her as a warm-blooded, feeling, and real human being; a woman of substance and passion. Nonetheless, some qualities can be inferred. For example, when Clare writes in her Form about the obstinate sisters and those who carried the business of the convent into the outer world, she well could have been speaking out of anger as well as concern. That she included it in her short rendition of a Rule seems to make it a matter of prominence in the daily experience of life at San Damiano. A purely empirical view of that section would not venture into possible conjecturing and a broader questioning of this text. A mythological hermeneutic is not satisfied with only looking at a text and story. It seeks to pierce through to the deeper possibilities present in the further questioning, "Yes, but what does it mean?" Therefore shored up not only by the depth psychological perspective of psycho-mythology, the topical study moved on to the next feature on the face of Clare's love, that of poverty.

Poverty is not a pretty picture and often 'smells' bad. The look of it is not usually associated with respectability or desirability. My academic search for poverty walked me through the negative realm of love where it is experienced as dark and painful, the agony that is partner to ecstasy. The study led me into an odyssey of reversals likened to the power of scents carried through the air where the smell may give lie to the flavor, or vice versa. Like some health herbs which smell bad but heal when ingested, so it is with poverty whose scent may be rank, but whose ingestion can be good for body and spirit. Clare and Francis passed through the odors of the avaricious rottenness around them and experienced an aroma beyond the first whiff, which resulted from taking that which is the rank and passing it through the atmosphere of their noses which could not be tricked. The scent of poverty became for them the aroma of the holy. That which is unacceptable in society, and this included lepers, became desirable to them. This reversal makes no sense to those who live life on a solely rational basis, or who think that they do.

A second apparent reversal appeared in the guise of simplicity of life. Clare and Francis were adamant that those who chose to follow their way accept the route of total material divestment of possession of land and goods. The testimony in church documents and writers of their day make it clear that such poverty was, in fact, practiced at San Damiano and among the original friars. However, I noted that history attests to the growth of the Franciscan way among those who were not clerics and professed religious. They were unable fully to divest themselves of possessions because of responsibilities to family. A simple form of life was given to them by Francis. Therefore poverty took on the trappings of simplicity of life, in which those who professed to be Franciscans were to live unspectacular and humble lives, practice Gospel principles, and use the things they needed for their lives and work with a sense of care and gratitude. Above all, to keep life as uncluttered and simple as possible to them. Poverty expanded to include the working poor and the generous rich. It took on a life of its own, changing to meet human needs.

Gaston Bachelard's theories concerning image as living symbol directed me toward mobile and fertile possibilities in the kingdom of poverty. Transformation can result from an honest encounter with a symbol. I believe that Clare may have held the burden of being Francis's feminine, breathing, human symbol of poverty. This theory would need much more focused study than I was able to give it in this dissertation. Nonetheless, it is one insight which emerged as I moved through my investigation of Franciscan poverty. If Clare was perceived as such an ideal, it would change the tenor, although not the actuality, of their relationship to one another. To hold the burden of being another person's ideal definitely constitutes a block in the development of a mature human relationship. Evidence of this barrier appears where marriages are entered with the notion of the ideal partner who will be the personification of one's ideal or dream image. One notable sign that such may not have been the case between Francis and Clare is in the succeeding section, where poverty is pictured as Lady Poverty, exclusive of Clare. However, as I worked through the section on poverty, it came to me as a possible part in a future study of their relationship. One fact remains: that the ideal which personified herself to Francis as a noble lady, was much like the Clare who became a living symbol to me as a woman in blue jeans and tee shirt. In the case of Francis, the personified ideal was important enough to change the course of the human relationship with creation, and, in my case, to consume two years of my precious later life.

The story of the fourth-century martyr Perpetua served to exemplify that smell penetrates the human psyche deeply enough to change the nature of an external experience from fear ridden to peaceful, and from ugly to beautiful. In a dungeon from where the young Perpetua and other Christians awaited their death in the arena at Carthage, she wrote of their wretched conditions in the dank prison confines. A co-prisoner named Saturus told Perpetua of a dream which he had. The young woman included it in her journal. The dream was set somewhere above the earth's atmosphere, where he and Perpetua stood in a garden-like place amid joyful people who presented them to a godlike man. It is not until the end of the story that the subject of scent is mentioned. It becomes significant because it is this memory of an indescribable fragrance which Saturus claimed held the power to sustain the entire company who peopled the dream, and which would sustain them through their persecution and ultimate death in the arena. Perpetua reports that the dream fragrance left Saturus filled with joy.

This story brought me to wonder and search out whether scent has powers far beyond the human reckoning. My past study of the living symbol led me to surmise that perhaps scent encompasses spirit much as the human spirit is embodied in flesh. Memory and imagination are spurred by the diversity of odors, some powerful enough to make the mouth water or cause a siege of nausea.

Clare wrote to Agnes of Prague that the fragrance of God "will revive the dead."

Nonetheless, Clare lived among the stench of lepers, the closeness of unbathed bodies, and the smells emanating from a rotting marshland. Poverty brought these odors into her immediate surroundings and challenged her to a new vision of wealth. I began to understand that Clare developed new sight. She saw that the God she loved remained present in all of creation: the ugly and the beautiful, the acrid and the fragrant and everything between. It is the new insight which drew her to love and appreciate creation, especially manifested in human nature. The way to that vision involved loneliness and courage. The one person who most shared that journey, Francis, died twenty-seven years before Clare breathed her final breath at age sixty. Alone in holding to a poverty which demanded divestment and dependence upon God, her confrontations with the ecclesial powers endured until her death. Clare's poverty would stand as the one shining gift to be left to the Church and the world, both of which insisted that living without the claim on any person or possession in this world is an impractical, if not impossible, feat. Not so. Clare and her small community at San Damiano birthed a new way of life. Once born, it became possible for future generations.

Finally, the reality emerged that poverty, both as simplicity of life and total divestment, are symbols of living freedom. Although love claims center stage in the production of Clare's story, poverty is a supporting actor, whose scent permeates the air throughout the entire theater of her life. The members of the audience determine whether they consider it foul or pleasing. Clare sniffed love in it, changing poverty from outsider to insider, much to the confusion and chagrin of many who still hold it in disdain.

In Search of Love

The section "The Mouth of Love," employs myth more directly than the preceding sections. The evasive character of love lent itself to the theme of search. Poets and scholars have wrestled with love's ever changing face and behaviors. Once named and captured in the articulation, love's shape shifts and escapes confinement. The Face of Clare's Love is not an exception.

The scholar, David Bona, seeks to understand the dreams of Francis of Assisi from a depth psychological perspective. In his dissertation entitled, 'The Dreams of St. Francis of Assisi: A Depth Psychological Study', Bona traces the history of western dream interpretation from biblical times, through the Church Fathers, and into the Middle Ages medieval period. He then distinguishes between his choice of a modern depth psychological approach and the theological/spiritual perspectives of the Biblical and medieval times. Using Bona's approach but not his topic, I placed the study of Clare's love within the context of mythology, emphasizing that this section of the dissertation would employ legends and stories unique to Clare and inclusive of Francis. The first of these stories was

"The Sacred Exchange between St. Francis and Lady Poverty."

The title of this story suggests that it belongs to the topic of "The Touch of Poverty." However, the tale portrays the passion of a lover in pursuit of the beloved. Francis seeks out the evasive Lady Poverty first by asking the poor where she might be. After receiving no help from them he goes to the rich and educated, who show not only surprise at his taking on such a venture, but also scorn Francis for even wanting to do so. This reminded me of the same kind of search described in the opening pages of the biblical book, "The Song of Solomon," a graphic and poetic story of love's yearnings, struggles, and final union. This mythical theme of Amor and Psyche reappears in Francis's passionate pursuit of Lady Poverty. I perceived that "The Sacred Exchange" appropriated itself to the topic of love. That is where it was placed.

The question was raised as to whether an allegory belongs to the family of mythology. Based upon a broad understanding of myths as being symbolic and fictional representations of timeless and universal human themes, I used this allegory to portray the ageless theme of love's determination and struggle to unite with the object of that love. Strictly interpreted, myths do not moralize and teach lessons. However, the hurdles of didacticism and moralization within the later context of this allegory posed no problem when seen in the extended light of other tales included in the genre of mythology, such as fairy and folk tales, both of which may contain lessons and morals.

The passion with which Francis wooed Lady Poverty was the same passion with which Francis, for a year previous to her running away from home to join him and his brothers, pursued the young Lady Clare Offreduccio.

The fire of their desires and longings united in falling in love with a Love beyond themselves, which held the potential to melt their own hearts into one. They were united in more than a task; they were one in heart, mind, and purpose. In depth psychological terms, it might be said that they manifested the outer constellation of one another's inner anima and animus. In today's terms, they were the perfect match. But I wondered how their relationship differed from any other which appears to be "the perfect match."

Perhaps a mutual passion for God and a marked devotion to God's service motivated Clare and Francis to find their clearest path to the Divine. This adds a nuance of mutuality to the relationship. For them, poverty became the road. Union with Love constituted the destination toward which poverty would lead them. After reflecting upon the quality of love between these two very passionate human beings, I arrived at a juncture in my study where theology with its emphasis on issues of divinity in relationship to humanity, or spirituality with its concentration on the intangible and nonmaterial could take me more deeply into an understanding of the unique love between these soul mates. However, I had set the limits of this study. Theology and spirituality were not included within those boundaries. Therefore I looked to legends as another means of embodying the loving exchange of intimacy between Clare and Francis.

The theme of presence-in-absence is shown through a vision which Clare shared with Sister Filippa, who in turn narrated the story at the canonization process. In the vision, Clare nurses at the breast of Francis. This told me that the nurturing quality of their friendship was mutual, that there was a reverse gendering process which occurred in their relationship in which feminine and masculine roles were interchangeable. I wondered at the respect and nonthreatening quality that such a love likely generated within their friendship. I noticed that in "The Sacred Exchange" Francis took on the role of the Shulamite woman in the biblical book "The Song of Solomon," one who frantically sought her lover and eventually found him. It may be true that love in theory may be genderless. However, it generally manifests within the context of well-defined cultural boundaries. In the case of Clare and Francis it simply jumped back and forth over the lines of gender roles during their own lifetimes.

Closeness in absence is shown in the legend, "The Face in the Well," which displays Francis's concern that Clare be happy and peaceful in her life. The writer narrates that while walking the road with Brother Leo, the companions stop at a well for refreshment. Francis is deep in thought, worried over Clare's wellbeing. He bends to look into the well, and there he sees Clare's serene countenance reflected upon the water looking back at him. At the end of this legend a relieved and joyful Francis exclaims, "After God and His Heavens-Clare!", a revealing comment in terms of the unique quality of his love for Clare.

A grand cave opens as I now consider and reflect upon my investigation of the love between Francis and Clare in the section, "The Mouth of Love." I stand at its dark opening with the light of new appreciations and understandings of Clare's place in history, in the Franciscan way of life, and in my personal relationship to her. I have looked into meanings woven through the fabric of a few of the legends written about Clare and Francis and found evidence of contrasexual influences present in their friendship like that of a man nursing a woman or a child suckling at the mother's/father's breast, both within the vision of Clare. "The Rose" narrates a tale which could be seen as a meeting of lovers symbolized by the flower of Aphrodite bursting into full blossom in the presence of this pair. The rosebush bows to the unfolding presence of love, acknowledging its power from an earthly plant-body point of reference. However, I remain curious as to the incorporation of the human body into the totality of their friendship.

The bond between Francis and Clare as incorporating an imagined sexual union within the context of a subtle body experience has not been built into this study. This dissertation is limited to Jung's basic notion of soul as explicated by Wolfgang Giegerich, a depth psychological approach which incorporates mythology, and active imagination as used by J. Marvin Spiegelman in his psycho-mythological approach. The fact remains that from my new knowledge of Clare's view that all is sacred, sexuality takes on an aura of the holy. Yet this most vibrant and vitalizing energy is neglected or underplayed in her. Whether this comes from shame, taboo, fear, or disdain remains in question. Certainly, research on the feudal attitude toward sexuality plays an important part in understanding the subject of sex as it was viewed by Clare and Francis. However, such a study is beyond the limits of this dissertation. As a point of clarification, I am not suggesting that she and Francis bedded together, but I am wondering if some of the dreams and visions which were of a more sexual nature were destroyed or yet remain to be found in dusty archives. My curiosity may be scoffed at by some, but it remains a fact that Clare of Assisi was a passionate woman in love with God, Francis, creation, and her sisters and brothers the world over. She was not disembodied. Experiences of the subtle body type are not off limits to persons who have reached her stage of spiritual awareness. They would be quite minor to a woman of Clare's extraordinary spiritual giftedness. However, to embark upon the treacherous seas of present society's rigidity or morbidity concerning the subject of sex, might prove to be a very perilous adventure. Furthermore, my often repeated lament that Clare of Assisi is revered within the Catholic Church as the model of virtuous perfection could result in a controversy of "burn the witch" proportions. Now that the humanity of Clare is more evident to me, exhumed from her tomb of hagiographical trimmings, the possibility of an ongoing study intrigues me. Commenting from a more personal place, I wonder if my interest rises from venturing to make her more touchable to the twenty-first century, or more human according to my needs.

Effective Affection

Clare's love is not generic. Although the all-inclusive sisterly and brotherly love basic to Agape surely permeated her behaviors, there remained persons for whom Clare held deep affection. I want to include in her affections those persons not emphasized in this present document. I have come to see that the Clare I learned to know likely possessed a deep affection for her mother, Ortulana, who joined her daughter in later life, and her blood sister, Agnes of Assisi, who at age fifteen was the first woman to join Clare in her new endeavor. This particular aspect of Clare's affection is fertile soil for further research, particularly from the perspective of women's love for one another. The excerpts of the letters to Agnes of Prague included in the discussion of Clare's eyes of contemplation substantiate the personal and warm relationship between these women, embodied in words filled with sentiment and affection. I believe that a prominent subject of her affection was Francis Bernadone. This was shown to be more apparent in the stories and legends found in the formal documents of the Process of Canonization, her Rule, and her Testament. Nonetheless, Clare's love flowed from out of the deep wells of her love for Christ.

The Long and Short of It

Clare's hagiographer wrote two pages about her. I wrote two hundred pages and still hope to find new understandings of this woman. She is known as mystic, saint, holy woman, and foundress. I am content calling her a human being to whom life was enough in itself. Being part of the totality of the created universe, diverse in its beauty and infinite in its forms, all was sacred to Clare and deserving of respect and care. Clare's last words clearly expressed what she herself thought of being human. In her final precious breathes Clare simply and gratefully stated, "I thank you for my life."

I am content to follow to its source
Every event in action or in thought;
Measure the lot; forgive myself the lot!
When such as I cast out remorse
So great a sweetness flows into the breast
We must laugh and we must sing,
We are blest by every thing,
Every thing we look upon is blest.

William Butler Yeats
(last two verses of 'A Dialogue of Self and Soul',
Bly, Hillman, and Meade, eds. 505-06)

When love breaks open the heart,
then I see that you who are you, is me.

BF

Works Cited

Armstrong, Regis J., ed. and trans. *Clare of Assisi: Early Documents.* Mahwah: Paulist, 1988.

Armstrong, Regis J. and Ignatius C. Brady, eds. *Francis and Clare.* The Classics of Western Spirituality. Ramsey: Paulist, 1982.

Armstrong, Regis J., J. A. Wayne Hellmann, O.F.M.Conv and William J. Short, O.F.M., eds. *Francis of Assisi: Early Documents.* 3 vols. New York: New City, 1999.
- *Francis of Assisi, The Founder.* Vol. 2. New York: New City, 2000.
- *Francis of Assisi, The Prophet..* Vol.3. New York: New City, 2001.
- *Francis of Assisi, The Saint.* 'The Sacred Exchange between St. Francis and Lady Poverty'. Vol 1. New York: New City, 1999.

Asher, Charles. *The Contemplative Self.* Big Sur: New Camaldoli, 1996.

Augustine, Saint. *St.Augustine Confessions.* Trans. Henry Chadwick. Oxford: Oxford, 1991.

Bach, Lester, O.F.M. Cap. *Catch Me a Rainbow Too: The Franciscan Journey.* Lindsberg: Barbo-Carlson, 1999.

Bachelard, Gaston. *On Poetic Imagination and Reverie.* Trans. Colette Gaudin. Dallas: Spring, 1971.

Bargellini, Piero. *The Little Flowers of Saint Clare.* Trans. Fr. Edmund O'Gorman, O.F.M. Cap. English translation with permission of Messaggero Editions Padua, Italy. Assisi, Italy: Edizioni Porziuncola, 1998.

Barks, Coleman. Trans. with John Moyne. *The Essential Rumi.* Edison: Castle, 1997.

Bataille, Georges. *The Absence of Myth: Writings on Surrealism.* Trans. Michail Richardson. New York: Verso, 1998.

Bly, Robert, James Hillman, and Michael Meade, eds. *The Rag and Bone Shop of the Heart: A Poetry Anthology.* New York: HarperPerennial, 1993.

Bona, David. 'The Dreams of St.Francis of Assisi: A Depth Psychological Study'. Diss. Pacifica Graduate Institute, 1996.

Braxton, Earl. 'Too Far in Us, Too Far Out, "Finding" and "Losing" One's Boundaries'. Leadership for Change: Chaos, Complexity, Resistance . . . and Courage Seminar. USD, San Diego. 12-13 July, 2002.

Bulfinch, Thomas. *Bulfinch's Mythology.* New York: Benetta A. Cerf and Donald S. Klopfer, Modern Library, 1936.

Butler, Alban. *Butler's Lives of the Saints.* 'St. Clare of Assisi' Vol. 3. New York: Kenedy & Sons, 1956.

Campbell, Joseph with Bill Moyers. Betty Sue Flowers, ed. *The Power of Myth*. New York: Doubleday, 1988.

Carney, Margaret O.S.F. *The First Franciscan Woman: Clare of Assisi and Her Form of Life*. Quincy: Franciscan, 1993.

Chittister, Joan, O.S.B. *The Rule of St. Benedict: Insights for the Ages*. New York: Crossroad, 2000.

Clare Agnes, O.S.C. *Clare Writes: The Four Letters of St. Clare in Miniature*. Arundel, Sussex: Convent of Poor Clares, 1992. N.pag.

De Robeck, Nesta. *St. Clare of Assisi*. Milwaukee: Bruce, 1951.

Doty, William G. *Mythography: The Study of Myths and Rituals*. Tuscaloosa: U of Alabama, 1986.

Downing, Christine. *The Goddess: Mythological Images of the Feminine*. New York: Continuum, 1996.
- *Myths and Mysteries of Same-Sex Love*. New York: Continuum, 1989.
- *Women's Mysteries*. New York: The Crossroad Publishing Company, 1992.

Edinger, Edward. *Anatomy of the Psyche-Alchemical Symbolism in Psychotherapy*. Chicago: Open Court, 1996.

- *Ego and Archetype*. New York: Penguin, 1972.

Fortini, Arnoldo. *Francis of Assisi.* New York: Crossroad, 1992.

Frances Theresa, Sister, O.S.C. *The Living Mirror.* Maryknoll: Orbis, 1995.

Fry, Timothy, O.S.B., ed. *RB 1980 The Rule of St. Benedict in Latin and English with Notes.* Collegeville: Liturgical, 1981.

Gibson, Audrey, and Kieran Kneaves. *Companions for the Journey: Praying with Louise de Marillac.* Winona: St. Mary's, 1995.

Giegerich, Wolfgang. *The Soul's Logical Life.* New York: Peter Lang, 1998.

Green, Julien. Trans. Peter Heinegg. *God's Fool: The Life and Times of Francis of Assisi.* New York: Harper & Rowe, 1985.

Grosso, Michael. *The Millennium Myth: Life and Death at the End Time.* Wheaton: The Theosophical Publishing House, 1995.

Guggenbuhl-Craig, Adolf. *The Old Fool and the Corruption of Myth.* Trans. Dorothea Wilson. Dallas: Spring , 1991.

Guider, Margaret Eletta, OSF, ed. *Doing What is Ours To Do: A Clarian Theology of Life.* Ashland: BookMasters, Inc., 2000.

Habig, Marion A., ed. *St. Francis of Assisi: English Omnibus of Sources for the Life of St. Francis.* Quincy: Franciscan, 1991.

Hillman, James. *Archetypal Psychology.* Dallas: Spring, 1983.
   - *Kinds of Power.* New York: Doubleday, 1995.
   - *Revisioning Psychology.* New York: Harper & Rowe, 1975.
   - *The Soul's Code.* New York: Pandom House, 1996.

Hone, Mary Francis, O.S.C., gen. ed. *Clare of Assisi: A Medieval and Modern Woman,* Ed. Ingrid Peterson. Clare Centenary Series 8. St. Bonaventure: Franciscan, 1996.

Horgan, Thaddeus. *Turned to the Lord.* Pittsburgh: Franciscan Federation of the Brothers and Sisters of the United States, Inc., 1987.

Jeffers, Robinson. *Selected Poetry of Robinson Jeffers.* New York: Random House, 1959.

Jung, Carl Gustave, *Memories, Dreams, Reflections.* New York: Random House, 1963
   - 'Aion'. *The Collected Works.* Trans. R. F. C. Hull. Ed. William Mcguire. Vol. 9, Pt. II. Bollingen Series 20. Princeton: Princeton U P, 1969.
   - 'Conscious, Unconscious, and Individuation'. *The Collected Works of C. G. Jung.* Trans. R. F. C. Hull. Vol. 9, Pt.1. Bollingen Series 20. Princeton: Princeton U P,1968.

Karper, Karen, P.C.P.A. 'Clare of Assisi: Spiritual Guide'. *Review for Religious* 48 (1989): 751-59.

Kerenyi, C., and C. G. Jung. *Essays on a Science of Mythology*. Trans. R. F. C. Hull. Bollingen Series XXII. Princeton: Princeton U P, 1978.

Kinsley, David R. *Hindu Goddesses - Visions of the Divine Feminine in the Hindu Religious Traditions*. Berkeley and Los Angeles: U of California, 1988.

Lainati, Sister Chiara Augusta, O.S.C. *Saint Clare of Assisi*. Trans. Sister Jane Frances, P.C.C. Assisi: Edzioni Porziuncola, 1994.

Lewis, C. S. *Till We Have Faces*. San Diego: Harcourt Brace & Company, 1980.

Mary St. Paul, Sister, P.C.C. *Clothed with Gladness-- The Story of St. Clare*. Huntington: Our Sunday Visitor, 2000.

Mayeski, Marie Anne. *Women Models of Liberation*. Kansas City: Sheed & Ward, 1988.

Miller, David. *Christs*. New York: Seabury, 1981.
- *Hells and Holy Ghosts: A Theopoetics of Christian Belief*. Nashville: Partheon,1989.
- 'Looking Glass'. *The Salt Journal* 2.1 (1999): 64.

Peifer, Rev. Claude, O.S.B. 'Decline and Renewal: the RB from the Thirteenth Century to Modern Times'. *RB 1980 The Rule of St. Benedict in Latin and English with Notes*. Ed. Timothy Fry, O.S.B. Collegeville: Liturgical, 1981.

Neumann, Erich. *Amor and Psyche.* Trans. Ralph Manheim. Bollingen Series 54. Princeton: Princeton U P, 1956.

Payne, Richard. J., ed. in chief. *Francis and Clare - The Complete Works.* Trans. Regis J. Armstrong, O.F.M. Cap. and Ignasius C. Brady, O.F.M. The Classics of Western Spirituality. New York: Paulist, 1982.

Peterson, Ingrid J. O.S.F. *Clare of Assisi - A Biographical Study.* Quincy: Franciscan, 1993.

Rice, Anne. *Interview with the Vampire: The Vampire Chronicles.* New York: Ballantine, 1976.

Rumi, Jelaluddin. *The Essential Rumi.* Trans. Coleman Barks with John Moyne. Edison: Castle Books, 1997.

Sabatier, P. *Mirror of Perfection.* New York: Charles Scribner's Sons, 1898.

Samuels, Andrew, and Bani Shorter, and Fred Plaut. *A Critical Dictionary of Jungian Analysis.* New York: Routledge, 1986.

Schlain, Leonard. *The Alphabet Versus the Goddess.* New York: Viking, 1998.

Schneiders, Sandra, I.H.M. *Selling All.* New York/ Mahwah: Paulist, 2001.

Sexson, Linda. *Ordinarily Sacred.* New York: Crossroads, 1982.

Sherman, Aliza Pilar. 'The Idol Life'. *Entrepreneur.*
January 2002: 55-57.

Sienkewicz, Thomas J. *Theories of Myth: An
Annotated Bibliography.* Lanham: Scarecrow, 1997.

Sisters of St. Francis of Assisi of Penance and
Charity. *Franciscans Gathered in Prayer,* Supplementary
Breviary. Milwaukee: Published by the Sisters of St.
Francis, 1998.

Slattery, Dennis Patrick, PhD, and Lionel Corbett MD.
eds. *Depth Psychology: Meditations in the Field.* Canada:
Daimon, 2000.

Spiegelman, J. Marvin, Ph.D. *Jungian Psychology and
the Passions of the Soul.* Las Vegas: Falcon, 1989.
- *The Tree--Tales in Psycho-Mythology.* Los Angeles:
Phoenix House, Inc., 1974.

Tanakh: The Holy Scriptures. Philadelphia: The
Jewish Publication Society, 1985.

*The American Heritage Dictionary of the English
Language.* 1970 ed.

Von Eschenbach, Wolfram. *Parzival.* Trans. A. T.
Hatto. New York: Penguin Books, 1980.

Von Franz, Marie-Louise. *Psyche and Matter.* Boston:
Shambhala, 1992.

Walker, Alice. *The Way Forward is with a Broken Heart*. New York: Random House, 2000

Whitmont, Edward C. *The Symbolic Quest*. Princeton: Princeton U P, 1991.

Weil, Simone. *Waiting for God*. Trans. Emma Craufurd. New York: Harper & Rowe, 1973.

Yeats, William Butler. 'A Dialogue of Self and Soul'. *The Rag and Bone Shop of the Heart: A Poetry Anthoogy*. Eds. Robert Bly, James Hillman, and Michael Meade. New York: HarperPerennial, 1993. 505-06.